Simple Grace

Also by Malcolm Boyd

Simple Grace

A Mentor's Guide to Growing Older

MALCOLM BOYD

Foreword by Martin E. Marty

Westminster John Knox Press
LOUISVILLE
LONDON • LEIDEN

Photographs courtesy of the Twentieth Century Archives Collection, Department of Special Collections, Boston University.

Book design by Sharon Adams
Cover design by designpointinc.com
Cover art: photo by Mark Thompson

First edition
Published by Westminster John Knox Press
Louisville, Kentucky

This book is printed on acid-free paper that meets the American National Standards Institute Z39.48 standard. ∞

PRINTED IN THE UNITED STATES OF AMERICA

01 02 03 04 05 06 07 08 09 10 — 10 9 8 7 6 5 4 3 2 1

Library of Congress Cataloging-in-Publication Data
Boyd, Malcolm, 1923–
    Simple grace : a mentor's guide to growing older / by Malcolm Boyd.
        p. cm.
    ISBN 0-664-22373-7 (alk. paper)
    1. Aged. 2. Aged—Conduct of life. 3. Middle aged persons—Conduct of life. 4. Aging—Psychological aspects. 5. Boyd, Malcolm, 1923– I. Title.
HQ1061 .B676 2001
                                                2001017705

To the Next Generation

Try to understand
who we were
where we have been
when we succeeded and when we failed
how we acted and reacted, and why

Blessings as you take the reins

CONTENTS

FOREWORD

$\mathcal{B}$oyd, Malcolm, minister, religious author, b. Buffalo, June 8, 1923. . . ." So reads *Who's Who in America*'s entry on the author of this book.

Let's see: 2001 minus 1923 means that Father Boyd will have turned seventy-eight in the year of this book's appearance.

Seventy-eight. Desmond Morris's *The Book of Ages* (New York: Viking, 1983) muses in terms that match those in *Simple Grace*:

> Seventy-eight is the year when the days seem to grow shorter. This strange, subjective phenomenon is first detected in middle age, but then intensifies in old age, especially in the late 70s, when many people get the feeling that life is slipping away faster and faster. This is elegantly summed up by Alice B. Toklas with the comment: "Dawn comes slowly but dusk is rapid."

Morris helps us locate people of Boyd's age with respect to achievements. The Ayatollah Khomeini used his seventy-eighth year to start the Iranian revolution. Author H. G. Wells finally got his D.Sc. degree. Charles de Gaulle retired. The seventy-eighth year was the last for Dwight Eisenhower and Mahatma Gandhi in Boyd's times and Kublai Khan and Tiberius before them. Dusk is rapid. Night falls. Boyd knows that and writes against the darkness.

Authors before this one have commented during their seventy-ninth year what it means to be seventy-eight. Near the end of this book Boyd takes an inventory of his body. Benjamin Franklin anticipates such stocktaking with a comment: "I still exist, and still enjoy some pleasures in that existence. . . . Yet I feel the infirmities of age come on so fast, and the building to need so many repairs, that in a little time the owner will find it cheaper to pull it down and build a new one." Franklin appears in Anthony and Sally Sampson's *The Oxford Book of Ages* (Oxford, 1985), the other book I use to mark the years.

Should Franklin's essay or Boyd's comments on creakiness be dispiriting, count on Boyd to be inspired and inspiriting as well. More of this book matches the tenor of Tolstoy cited in the Sampsons' book of ages than it does that of Franklin: "Don't complain about old age. How much good it has brought me that was unexpected and beautiful. I conclude from that that the end of old age and of life will be just as unexpectedly beautiful."

Simple Grace, while setting out to pose the author at his age and the reader at any age between the "down" and "up" comments just quoted, comes complete with a subtitle: *A Mentor's Guide to Growing Older*. This means that Boyd expects or hopes that we readers will be mentees—may I play with such a coinage in my mere seventy-third year?—who will take some sort of lessons about the process of aging from his progress. He fulfills the mentoring mission in numerous quiet asides. At other times he reminds himself that he is tutoring with end-of-chapter "How to . . ." comments, and even turns explicit with practical advice in a final chapter.

The mentor is named after Mentor, the Ithacan noble we meet in *The Odyssey*. Athena took on his disguise in order to quicken Telemachus to action and also to help lead Ithacans and Odysseus to make peace. From that word origin, I take it that the mentor does or may assume a disguise or a guise. Father Boyd's, from many angles, is obvious: he is a believer, a Christian, an Episcopalian, a priest, moved by "simple grace." But his mien has also been complicated. On these pages he recounts how for much of his life he had to disguise his homosexuality and do his mentoring as a straight, if sometimes tortured, man. And he reviews how he finally took off the mask and became himself, a mentor to many, especially Christians, who struggled with sexual and gender roles as he had.

William Sloan, a major editor-publisher, gave advice to autobiographers—and be not deceived, this is a second version of Boyd's autobiography—to the effect that people will not read "your" book simply because they are thinking, "Tell me about you." They are, instead, saying, whether explicitly or not, "Tell me about me, using yourself as the mirror." Trailing Malcolm Boyd by five years on the pilgrimage of grace, I found myself comparing notes on Depression childhood years, "the 50s" and "the 60s," and learning more about myself and my reactions by studying him and his.

Most readers of *Simple Grace* will not be men, Episcopal, gay, or authors. So Boyd's mirror may look clouded, off-angle, cracked and blurred. Never mind: it still offers perspective, sometimes especially to those who will find or feel themselves to be somehow "other," some way different. How, each might ask, does someone as different from me as Boyd is experience God and grace, or God as grace? What does this tell me about how my experience and witness match those of other ages and sorts and styles? What can I accept and what must I reject?

My wife and I took a walk some months ago and reviewed our decades. Would we prefer the whole complex of our lives as adolescents, as young people, or as middle-aged people to the way we get to live now? Both of us have known "unexpected and beautiful" times and things in graced abundance. We have known sorrows; we were both widowed. We both experience not onsets of creakiness, but signals of what a comment affixed to an X-ray of my spine said of its nether regions: "Shows the normal deterioration of a person his age." After inventorying, we answered our question: No—despite deteriorations, we would not prefer the "whole complex" after dawn to the time toward dusk.

The one thing we did not welcome, as Boyd does not welcome it, is that death is decades nearer than it was decades ago, to put the stark reality in as banal terms as possible. Yet Boyd serves as mentor when he deals with the end of the life we now know.

As I read him, I thought again of the last aria in

Leoš Janáček's opera *The Makropulos Affair.* The hero-
ine who sings it, though she is over three hundred
years old, remains the most beautiful woman and the
best singer in the world. For generations she has been
privileged to drink an elixir that fends off aging and
death. Now the recipe is gone and there will be no
more elixir, no more drinking, no more insulation
against death. The problem is that behind the mask
of her beauty is a wholly vain, utterly corrupt,
supremely bored person. Everything has happened
to her and nothing matters to her. Living or dying,
she sings, it's all the same to her.

Then she turns to those around her and sings of
her envy of the rest of the human race, who get to die
on schedule, as it were. She almost sounds like the
psalmist who asks the divine Mentor: "So teach us to
number our days, that we may apply our hearts unto
wisdom." She tells them that because of their immi-
nent end they also get to do what she cannot: they
can appreciate and celebrate "humanity, achieve-
ment, and love." In their mortality they become,
without their asking or necessarily wanting to be, our
mentors. Malcolm Boyd appreciates and celebrates
what they get to be, and what he wants to be—a
mentor. And, if we let him be, he is; so there is "unexpected beauty" ahead on these pages and in our lives.

MARTIN E. MARTY

ACKNOWLEDGMENTS

I want to thank:

The people who have lived and shared life with me. The book is as much theirs as mine.

Selected friends and associates who kindly read parts of the manuscript in its various stages of development and offered counsel.

David M. Dobson, one of the finest editors I have known, for steering the course and sharing the vision of the book.

Mark Thompson, for abiding wisdom and support.

INTRODUCTION

$\mathcal{T}$he themes of this book—Learning, Remembering, Simplifying, Maturing, Exploring, and Understanding—are major ones of my own life.

My fifties seemed the toughest time for me. I was forced to acknowledge that I hadn't yet found myself. Major changes in life lay ahead. The specter of aging was unpredictable, often scary. I asked: Must I deal with this *now?* The unmistakable answer was *yes.*

Moving gradually and slowly into uncharted territory, I sought directions. Could I find a map? make reservations somewhere? Where was I going? Could I pinpoint a destination?

I feel that I've become a seasoned, as well as scarred, survivor during the intervening years. I have explored hills and valleys of aging, crossed rivers, rested in meadows, engaged in dialogues, listened intently, worked hard, and met remarkable women and men. I sought wisdom and serenity above silver and gold.

Why should the story of my odyssey concern you? Because it is your story too. All our stories are interconnected and share common themes. The point is: always we are in the process of growing up. We need and can help one another by exchanging ideas, experiences, sorrows, joys, and certainly dreams and hopes. Willa Cather wisely observed that each person not only has a story, but often seems to have *become* his or her story. This is storytelling time.

Chapter One

LEARNING

*B*ut one thing took root in me—the conviction
that morality is the basis of things, and that truth is the
substance of all morality. Truth became my sole objective.
— Mohandas K. Gandhi

Marilyn Monroe, preserved on film, is eternally sexy.
Judy Garland is forever young Dorothy in Oz,
Vivien Leigh a nubile Scarlett, and James Dean a
youthful antihero. Laurence Olivier and Merle
Oberon are eternally doomed lovers in *Wuthering
Heights*, matched by Olivia de Havilland and
Montgomery Clift in *The Heiress*. If Cary Grant, Ava
Gardner, Clark Gable, and Lana Turner never grow
old, why must we?

Catching a sudden glimpse of myself reflected in a
store window the other day, I was shocked. I
appeared to be on the older side, stout, slightly bent
over, and not a quintessential image of virility and
sophistication.

I told myself: I don't look like that. I do, of course.
Why should I find difficulty in adjusting to the reality of that actual image? I'm sure one reason is the

sheer difficulty of trying to locate, and like, myself amid the jarring, conflicting images of an exaggerat-edly youth-oriented culture. Another, and related, factor may be all those permanent, never-changing images of long-deceased or quite elderly entertain-ment celebrities who remain eternally young on the videos we watch faithfully in our homes.

Yet it is essential in our never-ending learning process for survival to replace fantasy with reality. While Gary Cooper and Audrey Hepburn do not grow old on film, the rest of us certainly do in real life.

None of us, however, can assume—whether we're thirty, fifty, or seventy—that we have really learned *how* to live. This process involves so many diverse factors: relationships, self-esteem, empathy, aware-ness and use of skills, understanding and handling of feelings, a capacity to forgive and love, a grasp of what's essential, and a sense of transcendence.

"I have a good life, but in the still hours of the night I can't help wondering what it's all been for," someone wrote me. "I wish I knew I've had some rea-son for being on this planet. I'm a very ordinary per-son with only average intellect, no great talents or abilities. But I don't want to depart this life without having left at least a footprint."

This expresses a near-universal yearning for mean-ing. Can we find it? Where can we learn how?

While I've had to learn any number of lessons through the decades of my life, I have been fortunate to have splendid teachers. Mentoring, unselfishly offered by others, has frequently shown me the way to move ahead more wisely and with needed grace.

For example, I used to be a slave to perfectionism. Imperfections of others could stir my ire as if it were a pot of witches' brew. It was, therefore, startling for me to see perfectionism shattered casually with a single blow by one of my life's teachers, theologian Reinhold Neibuhr, one day in New York City in 1956. I was a graduate student at Union Theological Seminary and he was my tutor.

Niebuhr's secretary walked into the room where we were talking, carrying a copy of an article he'd written for a journal. The piece was freshly typed for an immediate deadline. "It isn't very good, is it?" he asked her. His secretary paused for a moment, then said quietly, "No, it isn't." "Mail it," he replied. Surprised, I saw this distinguished public figure give his pride short shrift, professionally (and kindly) meet his deadline, and humbly deal a knockout blow to perfectionism.

Many years later, just when I figured I had mellowed to near perfection—how dangerous it was to do this!—I experienced one of my life's worst crises around the expectation of perfectionism. It involved a close friendship. You see, a friend and I had both taken it for granted. We were as comfortable with our friendship as if it were an old garment one loved to wear.

Our mutual expectations, however, grew out of proportion to reality. Suddenly, we saw clearly that our friendship was imperfect. I guess we found this intolerable—or scary—when it led to an explosive, painful argument. As the smoke cleared, we had become grumpy old men in the worst possible scenario or stereotype. An armistice was called for. Who could be the peacemaker?

That task fell to both of us. It was a humbling and instructive experience. We came to realize that ours was a deeply familial sort of bonding that must be accepted on its own terms. This meant, of course, it would never be perfect. It would remain—as are all the best things in life—flawed, challenging, and full of promise. For us, an opportunity emerged for a stronger, sturdier friendship.

In other parts of my life I've been alarmed to see, from time to time, that I have allowed my self-image to become separated from my real self. In other words, I've chosen to view myself as accepting, mentoring, helpful, and very, very wise, when I wasn't. These were times, once again, for me to shape up.

This usually involved giving up control. Getting out of the way. Diminishing ego.

> Riding the crest
> of a fast-flowing stream
> it occurs to me
> something remarkable
> has taken place
>
> I have given up
> control

Letting go of something we want, when we really ought to let go of it for the sake of others as well as ourselves, requires both wisdom and courage. Once I was the head of a powerful volunteer organization that had started out with pioneering efforts in a crucial area of public service. After several years, primary objectives had been achieved, with the result that both crucial need and a sense of passion in our activity had disappeared.

We refused to acknowledge that we had become just another layer of bureaucracy. To make matters even more complicated, I refused to admit that I had come to enjoy the power of my position and its perks. The real truth was: the organization had changed to *my* organization. It was crippled in sterility as an outpost of empire.

A friend told me the truth. In an honest moment of self-reflection and truth-seeking, I offered to resign—get out of there—for everybody's sake, including my own. I was enabled to see clearly that fresh blood was needed, with a brand-new vision and different leadership.

Yet, at the same time, it hurt me a great deal to surrender my imperial trappings. I asked: Hadn't I earned them the hard way? In fact, didn't they belong to me? Thank God, I was granted the grace to step down. Soon, the organization shifted to a new plateau and found stability, motivation, and new goals.

At other times, however, I have found that letting go is not the problem. Instead, it's adding a new duty, shouldering a different task. Usually this occurs at a moment (in any of our lives) when we really don't wish to do it—yet perhaps, more instinctively, we feel some kind of moral obligation to go ahead. What if no one else is on the horizon to accept this responsibility? Then, if it dawns on us that it has become our responsibility, how can we justify turning away and saying no?

I recall when I found myself in precisely this situation. A classic type of "thankless" task was offered to me. Unquestionably, it needed to be done. Yet it was a "no win" situation, clothed from head to toe in controversies. Misunderstanding and misinterpretation were everywhere. I centered myself, quieted down internally, spent a lot of time in meditation, and pondered my role.

Slowly I realized that I could do it. In time I decided that I *should*. When I did, my life took on a brighter zest because I knew this mattered deeply. My initial selfishness and desire to remain uninvolved had given way to a greater good. Yet it bothered me that I had stood back and waited, partially from that old primordial fear of getting up in front of everybody and taking an unequivocal stand.

Another hard lesson I had to learn is not to fear— or reject as a knee-jerk reaction—new ideas that appear to be disturbing and threatening. (It can seem so much easier to close the door on them.) Sadly, rejecting them can also mean preventing creative change from taking place in our own lives.

Two small signs appear on my office door. One says: "Fear No Art." The other says: "Fear No Art." What's the point? The first reminds us not to fear art that challenges us and makes a demand on us to think differently. The second tells us to fear the absence of art.

I am grateful to those life teachers who have taught me by their positive examples. I would be remiss, however, if I failed to thank those life teachers who have illuminated my consciousness and instructed me by means of their negative examples. Some were alcoholics who did not seek healing and damaged other people's lives, including my own.

Some were public demagogues and professional haters—racists, anti-Semites, homophobes.

A few were mega-successful men and women who cultivated images of glamour and untouchable fame, yet privately sacrificed their companions, children, loved ones, associates, and employees on a private altar dedicated to narcissism and power at any cost.

A legendary actress, who was once one of the most beloved women in the world, played a major role in my life, teaching me far more by her failures than her success. Mary Pickford, with Charlie Chaplin, launched global entertainment celebrity in the twentieth century, and she was the first great woman star.

At the age of twenty-five I became her partner in the production company PRB, Inc. Mary had reigned as empress of Hollywood with her movie-star husband Douglas Fairbanks and been known universally as "America's Sweetheart."

Joining Mary in the work arena, I moved into a fantasy world I had only dreamed of, a sphere of seemingly unlimited power and privilege. Everything was outwardly gorgeous, so it seemed fitting that the only photograph in Mary's lavish reception room was that of designer Elsie De Wolfe, also known as Lady Mendl.

Dinners hosted by Mary were often like state occasions. Big parties on the lawn were spectacular. From the immense, kidney-shaped pool one could look out over Beverly Hills and down at Doris Duke's Falcon's Lair, which had once been the home of Rudolph Valentino. Queen Marie of Romania and

I learned how to swim in the pool at Pickfair, a scene of incredible glamour that was once second only to the White House as a famous home. Here, royalty and stars mingled quietly, far from the public eye.

England's Lord Mountbatten had slept in the jewel-like guest house, where I often stayed on visits.

My life resembled an amusement park roller-coaster ride, complete with stars, glamour, and luxury. I enjoyed (or, at least, was dazzled by) it for a while. Yet, as I looked into the future, this was neither the life I wanted nor what I wished to become.

In 1951, I left PRB, Inc., and departed Hollywood to enter an Episcopal seminary and prepare to become a priest. My going-away party at Ciro's was funny—without our intending it to be—when, as columnist Hedda Hopper wrote, everybody (including the bartender) lowered their heads during the recitation of the Lord's Prayer.

Off I went to seminary and a quite different life. Mary and I remained close during the years that followed. Once, when Mary was cochair of a national bond drive with First Lady Mamie Eisenhower, she visited San Francisco for a few days. I came over from my seminary in Berkeley to spend several days with her in the suite of her hotel. We rode a cable car at night (Mary, in mink and jewels, startled the other riders) and slipped away for a classic Italian dinner at an unfashionable restaurant.

Her visit ended on a macabre note for me, however, when she visited my seminary as an honored guest for dinner. The moment had come for my classmates to meet my old friend from Hollywood. It meant a lot to me. But Mary, who drank out of public view, took a secret drink too many that night— probably out of fear of seminarians and future priests, not knowing how precisely to handle her performance that time. She made a terrible, unforgettable scene. Her visit was a disaster. I was dumbstruck and wounded.

Here was Mary, someone with every resource at her fingertips to continue growing positively as a human being, going down the drain instead. Her drinking had become the oldest of stories for me. Often I had shared it with actress Lillian Gish, who continued working creatively in both theater and film and was an old friend of Mary. After Mary left her dinner table one night, Lillian and I went looking for her and found her on the floor of the guest house, where she had passed out. It seemed tragic that instead of offering her unique gifts to a world that awaited them, Mary became a recluse. Finally, she simply gave up and relinquished any reason to get out of bed in the morning. What happened? I believe she allowed her celebrity image to destroy her by becoming imprisoned in it. A woman in an iron mask, ravaged by alcohol and barely alive to the grace of living, Mary slid into a twilight zone.

Shortly before her death, Mary asked to see me. Pickfair, her home, had earlier rivaled the White House in fame. Now it was silent, deserted, as much an anachronism as the lonely castle in Orson Welles's celebrated film *Citizen Kane.* I climbed the spiral stairway to Mary's room.

She lay outstretched on her bed, nearly resembling a skeleton. Her emotion was unrestrained. She placed her tiny, frail hands around my waist, hugging me. She called me her spiritual son. We had long shared spiritual quests, though vastly different ones, taking different directions.

Now Mary spoke of God and the great pain she suffered. She said her veined hands were like a monkey's, but I told her my hairy hands were much more so. As we talked, I recalled happier times at Pickfair when, beautiful and elegant, Mary was a splendid storyteller who could charm anyone. Her sense of humor had been a marvel. President Franklin D. Roosevelt had even suggested she should run for the U.S. Senate.

Tears rolled down her face on this morning. She pointed to her father's and mother's photographs that hung on a wall. "Papa died when I was so young," she told me, "but I loved him just as much as Mama." After saying what would be my final good-bye to Mary, I left her room and walked down to the Pickfair swimming pool at the far end of the garden. Here, I had first learned how to swim. Now I stripped off my clothes and dived into the water. It was a ritual cleansing I sought.

It saddened me that I couldn't help Mary, who could seemingly have done virtually anything in her life that she wished. The problem was, she didn't wish. Mary's example was, I realized, a negative one. I saw her story as telling how *not* to live one's life.

She gave an appearance of having become a prisoner locked inside a cell. Had she locked *herself* inside? I wished she could have fled her castle one night under cover of darkness, flung away her crown, and found solace in a snug cottage with a hearth, a cat comfortably ensconced in a window seat, a kettle humming on a stove, and an uncluttered view of the sky from an open doorway.

Fondly, I shall always remember a particular life's scene I shared with Mary. In 1953, when I was still a seminarian, I spent the summer at the Mount Calvary Monastery in Santa Barbara. One day Mary traveled by car from Los Angeles to visit me.

The elderly prior had kindly invited her to join us for tea. Lacking resources to be a perfect host, he asked a local socialite to prepare a "proper tea." In awe of Mary's reputation, she wished to make an impression. She brought from her home a full silver service. She also overdressed and wore jewels.

I was in my twenties, and Mary Pickford had long been one
of the world's best-known celebrities, when we were partners in a
production firm, PRB, Inc. I left to become a seminarian at the
Church Divinity School of the Pacific.

Mary, on the other hand, deserved an Oscar for her performance as a beleaguered empress in a stark Byzantine drama in a monastic setting. She wore a simple dress, no jewelry except her wedding band, and, leaving her chauffeur in town, drove alone to the monastery nestled in the hills.

As the occasion moved forward, the socialite dropped the names of movie stars and members of the British royal family. An orphan in a storm, Mary sought peace in the person of the stately, white-robed prior. She was caught by his steady gaze, warmed by his resonant voice. When the socialite talked ever more stridently of dukes and queens, Mary's voice grew eloquently still. At last, almost in a whisper, she spoke only of God.

My learning continued apace.

"The Take-over Generation: One Hundred of the Most Important Young Men and Women in the United States" was announced by *Life* magazine in a special issue on September 14, 1962. No one on the list was over forty.

We were identified prominently by our age. The list included John Updike, 30; Leontyne Price, 35; Andre Previn, 32; Edward Albee, 34; Shirley Ann Grau, 33; Theodore Sorenson, 34; Mark Hatfield, 40; Harold Prince, 34. I was one of the oldest at 39.

Life said the "Red-Hot Hundred" were selected according to a rigid set of criteria. They had: (1) tough, self-imposed standards of individual excellence; (2) a zest for hard work; (3) a dedication to something larger than private success; (4) the courage to act against old problems; (5) the boldness to try out new ideas; (6) a hard-bitten, undaunted hopefulness about humanity.

I ask myself: What if a magazine planned now to announce the "'Red-Hot Hundred' Older Men and Women"? What criteria would be used to establish the list? Along with noteworthy accomplishments, I might suggest the following: A simple gracefulness. Pure nonchalance. A diminishing of ego. A still lingering innocence in the eyes. An unstudied smile. An inviting sense of warmth. A politically incorrect response to phoniness and hypocrisy. Inherent dignity. A certain gentleness. Humor that is mellow. A sense of self that lingers in a room after a person departs.

I might add these qualities: the ability to summon reserves of energy when these are in short supply; to change an angry debate to an intelligent discussion; to bring people together instead of driving them apart; to give, and receive, forgiveness; to turn the rigors of pride into signs of camaraderie, even community.

Responding to such a list, virtually anyone would probably come up with women and men who deserve to be nominated. One nominee of mine would be Jean Sharley Taylor Lescoe, one of the first women to hold a top editorial position at a major U.S. newspaper. Now retired, and one year younger than me, she has many interests, friends, beguiling charm, and wide-ranging wisdom.

"The concept of old age beginning at sixty-five is artificial," she told me. "Old age today is an attitude established by corporate America and accepted by society. Strangely enough, we choose Presidents who are older, along with senators and congressional representatives who head important committees when they are close to ninety. But why only in government?

"In my experience in newspapering, I was asked to encourage editors, even good ones, to leave at sixty-two or sixty-five because of their high salaries and pensions. Once when I refused to encourage a fine section editor to retire, this led to a heated discussion with the Metro editor. He said if he had his way he would dispatch everyone over sixty-two except the visible columnists.

"In my seventies, I am aware that our generation is really the first to push back the concept of aging. The life expectancy in 1900 was forty-three or forty-six. In 2000 it is seventy-nine for women, a few years under for men (delicate creatures). With medical and nutritional advances, it might be one hundred twenty by 2100."

I found Jean alert and sharp as a tack, much the same as when she was shepherding several sections of the *Los Angeles Times* while finding time to be a compassionate mother confessor to a score of editors and writers. I have long admired her poise, warmth, and changing beauty.

I remember a church pastor with equal affection. Always I stood in awe of him. He became a role model who influenced the course of my life. Paul Roberts, dean of St. John's Cathedral in Denver, was locked into a solid position in the establishment of his time, yet willingly accepted widespread criticism for his espousal of social-justice issues.

Softened majesty and warmth, innate dignity and

studied simplicity in any woman or man is a wonderful sight to behold. For me, it becomes a revelation of grace at whatever age it occurs. This is a redefinition of beauty that contradicts popular wisdom and celebrates the riches of the soul.

Dag Hammarskjöld seems to have caught the spirit of this when he wrote in *Markings*: "In a dream I walked with God through the deep places of creation: past walls that receded and gates that opened, through hall after hall of silence, darkness and refreshment—the dwelling place of souls acquainted with light and warmth—until, around me, was an infinity into which we all flowed together and lived anew, like the rings made by raindrops falling upon wide expanses of calm dark waters."

A few of my best teachers in life have been rather surprising ones. They have corrected my education when it went awry. They determinedly opened my eyes to reality and truth.

Looking back over the years, I realize it has taken the greater part of my life to unlearn what I was taught as a child. In schools, in churches and other institutions, people spoke earnestly of "educating" me. Yet I was taught about a world that either did not exist or should not have.

History was shoehorned into carefully arranged categories. For example, I was taught that war was justified if my country fought it.

I was taught that black people were simple fools, could be dangerous if confronted, and were called niggers behind their backs.

I was taught that native Americans were deadly,

monstrous creatures incapable of spirituality, who had killed kind and courageous (white) American troops fighting for "our country."

I was taught that Latinos were inferior louts who were always to be treated as children. Behind their backs one could mimic their speech and laugh uproariously.

I was taught—after Pearl Harbor—that Japanese Americans should be deprived of their human and civil rights, driven from their homes, punished by losing everything they owned, and herded into primitive camps where they would suffer.

I was taught that gay people (the word was homosexuals or faggots) were the lepers of our society, unspeakable in their demonology, cursed by God, destroyers of morality, and incurably sick people (usually pedophiles), incapable of loving.

I was taught that modern civilization was essentially good, light years ahead of the horrors of the Middle Ages. Then came the facts of the Nazi concentration camps during the Holocaust, as revealed in sworn testimony in the Nuremberg Trials: "The completely naked people went down a few steps. Then I heard a succession of shots. I looked in the trench and saw how the bodies twitched, blood spurted from their necks."

How was I to overcome the shortcomings of my education? Life took over as my teacher. A Rubicon was crossed in my own life when, in 1961, I was asked to participate in a prayer pilgrimage/freedom ride in Mississippi. In fact, my entire life was turned around.

I discovered a different America than I had known.

I saw startling new situations. I acquired new knowledge. Finally, despite my innate shyness, I found that I could do new things: take enormous risks, become a leader, adopt a confrontational style if necessary, and communicate without apology, frills, or fear.

New teachers appeared. One was Martin Luther King Jr. I was in his company on several occasions. One spring day in 1965 I was in Brown Chapel in Selma, Alabama, when he preached: "It's better to go through life with a scarred body than a scarred soul." So I was taught that ideals were possibilities. He knew the way toward justice, nonviolence, and peace would be an arduous one: "Pilate's great sin wasn't that he didn't know what was right but that he lacked the moral courage to stand up for right."

At a time when blacks and whites were moving away from one another on separate paths, he held up integration as essential. The last time I was in his company was during a nonviolent protest against the Vietnam War on February 6, 1968, in Washington, D.C. He urged that the answer to the racial dilemma can be discovered only in persistent trying, perpetual experimentation, and persevering togetherness. These remain the truest words I have ever heard on the subject.

New teachers—unknown ones, never famous— were emerging. A young African American man told me during the Watts rebellion in Los Angeles in 1965: "This isn't a race riot. It is letting out a yell saying, 'We're still living, we're here, you've got to let us live like you do.'"

In 1970 I stood with others in a circle at the national convention of a major Protestant denomination. We took turns reading aloud the names, published in the *Congressional Record*, of American casualties in Vietnam. Every half hour we knelt to pray silently, remembering also the Vietnamese war dead whose names we did not know. Suddenly, a middle-aged clergyman attending his church's convention broke angrily into the circle. "What has this to do with God?" he demanded.

Instantly, he became yet another of my life's teachers, a part of my continuing education. I realized if he did not know the answer to his question, the church had about as much chance to be a vital moral guide as a flickering candle had to survive in a hurricane.

And I learned how fragile security can be when, as a forty-year-old, white Episcopal priest, I stood guard at three A.M. in McComb, Mississippi, on October 1, 1964. My night watch outside a freedom house filled with white and black student volunteers in voter registration was to prevent a recurrence of an earlier dynamite explosion that had bombed an African American church. I tensed when I heard a sound—a dog bark, footsteps, a car on a road.

My education was continuing.

It still is. Now I feel a need to learn about death. While mortality is only a speck on the horizon, I want to be able to look at it clearly and honestly, without fear. I like author Colin Fletcher's suggestion that we should act as though we'll live forever, yet know we might die before lunch. This counsel applies to all of us, at any age.

When I was a boy and Laddie, my pet collie, was killed by a car, it broke my heart.

Then, a pal's untimely death while we were students in junior high school seemed cruel and rapacious. Why the hell, I asked, couldn't death stay out of the way and leave us alone?

Of course, I remember the big-time deaths when the demise of famous people made bold headlines. FDR had saved the country in the Depression, led us through World War II, and was into his fourth term as U.S. President when he died. It was a staggering public event. Everyone cried, or felt like it, because a universal father figure was gone. Glamour collided with pathos when film star Jean Harlow died tragically at twenty-six. Composer George Gershwin died of a brain tumor at thirty-eight. Folk icon Will Rogers was killed in a plane crash, and there was a sense of suffering in our collective life. The message was clear: Even the world's new breed of gods and goddesses was not immune to dying.

Before long, to my astonishment, more of my own friends began to die.

William dropped dead in the doorway of his Manhattan apartment late one night, having just returned from walking out to buy an early edition of the next morning's newspaper.

Janet died of Alzheimer's; so did Harry.

Kathy hanged herself in a closet adjoining her bedroom.

Laurent's heart, long a problem, quit on him.

Another friend died on the operating table during surgery. I had visited him in the hospital on the preceding day. We laughed and reminisced fondly about our student days together. He was as outrageous as he'd always been when it came to poking fun at what he felt was pomposity. In fact, I realized once again that he should really have given Noël Coward a run for his money by going on the stage. At the end of our long chat we embraced. I promised to telephone the next afternoon to find out about the surgery. When I did, they told me he had died.

I visited Gin shortly before her death, yet had no premonition of it. She set an elegant table for a dinner party in my honor on her wobbly front porch that could have been painted by Edward Hopper. Four of us dined there by candlelight as neighbors stole looks from nearby windows and moths swept into our hair. Gin was the Perle Mesta or Pamela Harriman of the evening, on fire with grace, poised, in command of the situation. We talked and sipped wine late into the night. It was just a few weeks later that I was notified that Gin had died, apparently quietly, in her bed at home.

Claude had long suffered a kidney disease and had been on dialysis for nearly a decade. During that time I frequently visited him. We talked and talked and talked. He was one of the wisest and kindest men I ever knew. Several years after I had moved to another city, Claude became aware he was dying. He sent me a round-trip plane ticket. Could I come to visit for the last time? I did. It was a rare, unforgettable occasion. I deeply mourned his death. I had lost an irreplaceable friend.

Paul Monette died of AIDS at forty-nine, two years after receiving the National Book Award for writing *Becoming a Man*. I had often swum beneath the branches of an elm tree by the pool of his house above the Sunset Strip in Los Angeles. Paul knew death was approaching. The two of us sat before the grate in his living room and talked about it. Paul truly yearned to live as much as anyone I've ever known. Yet, despite his passion for life, death was a presence in the room with us, unyieldingly beckoning to him. His was a life brutally cut short. I recall when I stood by his graveside on a grassy knoll, holding a shovel and thrusting a parcel of dirt on his casket in the grave.

After a number of personal encounters with death, I consider death as no longer a stranger at all. Death has become a regular boarder. I've grown accustomed to death's manners, laugh, personality quirks, attitudes, and stories spun after drinking a glass of red wine.

I like what Walt Whitman wrote in his poem "When Lilacs Last in the Dooryard Bloom'd":

> Come lovely and soothing death.
> . . . .
> praise! praise! praise!
> . . . .
> Have none chanted for thee a chant of fullest
>   welcome?
> Then I chant it for thee.

Why not? Isn't this the sanest, most mature and enlightened way to deal with death? Since death happens at twelve and twenty-four, at forty as well as sixty, at fifty as well as seventy, it is only sensible to be prepared for it at any time.

Still, while I have little or no objection to death, my personal message to death at this moment is: "Come around *next* time if you like. The door will be open. But if it's perfectly all right with you, why don't we skip *this* time? I'll be seeing you."

If I awaken during the night, I know exactly how to reach out my hand and turn on the lamp by my bed. Or if I approach the front door of my house in the dark, I never have to think twice about placing the key in the lock, and having it turn easily to open the door. These things are automatic, casual, easy.

While I have grown accustomed to many things, places, and people, still I recognize that I am living on borrowed time. This, while I am so comfortable with time and do not want it to run out.

The irony of this was caught in an ad for the TV miniseries *On the Beach*: "Tomorrow isn't coming. Today has to last a lifetime." Of course, we all know that today will become tomorrow, unless . . . Yet there is an element of universal truth in what the ad says. There comes a moment for any human being on earth when tomorrow *isn't* coming.

I found it touching when someone in Iris Murdoch's novel *Jackson's Dilemma* recalled his past, pondered his future (unknown to him), and asked himself a question: "*Had* he a future?"

For myself, my future on earth is consciously limited in terms of time. How do I try to deal with this knowledge? I do some "big" things, like concentrating on forgiveness, mending, healing, communicating, and loving.

There are several "smaller" ways:

Allow silences to expand as deep as they want to go.

Concentrate with a singular intensity, focus, on the sweeping branches of an ancient oak or the intricate mystery of a hibiscus blossom; move rhythmically into the flow of a stream of water, letting it divert the mind; savor a glimpse of the elusive first light of morning.

Listen to a favorite piece of music—say, the *Four Last Songs* of Richard Strauss—as if one might, just might, not hear it again.

Search resolutely for the meaning of something instead of casually surrendering it.

Take a closer look at anything, and hold it.

Shouldn't all of us really be doing this most of the time?

Chapter Two

REMEMBERING

When I turn and look behind me, I like to see where I have been.

—*Wright Morris*

Remembering is essential for me. After all, what is at stake is my life. I've lived it and continue to do so.

Memory is the continuing story that tells us who we are, where we've been, what we've done, and, perhaps most important, who has shared life's journey with us.

"Up to age twenty-one, my life was happy, protected, and filled with love," someone wrote me. "When I got married, and until my divorce, I had a very unhappy time, making painful memories. After that, I focused on my two children, working to support them. Now they are grown and have left home. Earlier, I had seemingly succeeded in blocking bad memories. But now I find that I cannot, because the trauma has come back in full force. I need healing for my anger and bad memories."

We can be helped by coming to an understanding of what lies in the past. "I try to reach back into my own history," someone else told me. "This lets me understand my mom and dad better, as well as where I came from, my family's story, and what made me the sort of person I am."

Anyone can write a personal memoir or some stories about his or her life in order to search for self-understanding as well as leave a legacy for others. A friend of mine wrote her grandmother's story, she said, in order to better understand her mother and herself. Keeping a journal and recording a history, or *her*story, provides an opportunity to reflect on the past and look closely at the present—its joys and sorrows, wins and losses, and inner feelings of the soul and heart.

My reminiscences about my family that follow are intended to stir or awaken your sense of memory. As you read these, whom do you remember from your past? Who touched, influenced, and helped shape your life?

Why, I wonder, do I remember my youthful and high school experiences far more vividly than later ones? I recall names of classmates, see their faces, and relive events. Elsie B. Essex was especially helpful to me in junior high school. Mary E. Lowe mentored me in high school. Duncan Emrich went out of his way to be incredibly useful as a mentor in college. They remain alive to me.

I learned a great deal about remembering from my mother during my visits to her in a convalescent hospital and nursing home during the several years before her death. Beatrice was unable to remember most people and events in her life during the past forty years, due to dementia. For example, she had no clear recollection of my father. Since her mind wandered a lot, I grew accustomed to having her tell the same story over and over, sometimes three times within a half hour.

Yet Beatrice's memory was absolutely clear when it came to her childhood in Cripple Creek, Colorado, when it was a gold-mining town. Since she spoke of it often, it became a familiar open book for me too. I relished her retelling of the same stories. One concerned an overnight visit she made to her girlfriend Clara's house, when Beatrice could not sleep because Clara's father snored loudly in the next room. Finally Beatrice slipped quietly out of the house and ran home to her own bed. I heard too about the pranks with her friend Agnes. And there was an indelible story about a familiar town figure, Dr. Hassenplug, who went for walks accompanied by his three dachsunds. Whenever he turned a corner, they followed him, unhurriedly moving in single file.

I could scarcely believe it when Mother remembered the most minute details of her stories: names, places, dates. Often they made her laugh. This provided her immense happiness and deep contentment. It allowed her to check out of present stress and difficulties, and dwell in a highly personal secret garden of her spirit. I watched as she seemed to become young again, reliving happy moments.

Do you remember a particular grandmother or grandfather? How did your grandparents influence

A boy from Manhattan, I visited Grandpa and Grandma in Texas after my parents divorced. Although rural life was new to me, I found both of them warm and fascinating.

your life? In your memory, were they close to you or distant? easy to understand or difficult to know? Did you love them? Why?

I can clearly remember Grandpa. He belonged to the old school. A man's man who had drilled for oil in India and now did the same in Texas, he was tall, had a ramrod back, and everybody called him Colonel.

Grandpa broached no nonsense, yet as a boy I discovered a twinkle in his eye. He had a soft spot for me, especially when he held me on his knee or took me with him out into the fields of rural Texas to climb up great tanks filled with oil.

His life embraced elements, however, that seemed brutally raw to me. I remember an afternoon when Grandpa was one of a group of men who slaughtered a pig. The pig, bleeding, ran squealing around a circle, hemmed in by men who were drinking liquor from bottles, stabbing at it with knives and hatchets, and laughing. The scene made an indelible impression on me, as one of horror and fear.

Grandpa had few words, being a man of action. Still, I perceived warmth and tenderness in him, particularly in the way he treated Grandma. He deferred to her. Married once before, in this union he seemed to have a practiced, harmonious, well-choreographed marriage. There were few, if any, surprises on the surface of it. He was the breadwinner, head of the household, gruff, somewhat remote in his manliness, seemingly secure in his role. He smoked a pipe, ate a full meal, and liked to reminisce, telling stories about his adventures in India.

I shall never forget his death, gargantuan in my eyes. Grandpa appeared larger than life as he lay in a large mahogany bed. Grandma sat by his bedside, gently sobbing. A doctor stood opposite her. Members of Grandpa's family, including children from his first marriage, crowded into the room. I hugged a rear corner, scared, yet drawn irresistibly to the unfolding drama. I was aware of the loss that his death would mean to me. Clearly, I was losing a special pal. A significant male figure was passing out of my life forever, and there would never be another like him.

Grandma was an indomitable woman who never gave up. She worked against the greatest odds, and kept trying, doing this with high humor and unerring spirit. She drove herself all her life, refusing to yield an inch to self-pity. She genuinely liked people.

Ruth, my grandmother, was a pioneer woman in many ways. After Grandpa's death, when the family's fortunes went down the drain in the Depression of the 1930s, Grandma rolled up her sleeves quite literally, working very hard in several different enterprises. When she met failure, she simply started all over again. Through all this, she never forfeited her ready smile or intrinsic optimism about life. Believing in the basic goodness of people, she was an implicitly spiritual woman more than an explicitly religious one. While she prayed faithfully and followed a rigorous ethical code, she abstained from membership in a church.

My fondest memory of Grandma goes back to a visit I paid my grandparents when I was a small boy. She suffered an unexpected pleurisy attack. While it wasn't serious, it was considerably painful. Grandma was a carefully rational person on most occasions, yet this time she may have just been in the mood for a scene of high drama. So, quite uncharacteristically, she seemed to prepare for her own Camille-like deathbed act.

A doctor, arriving hurriedly, knew immediately what to do. He prescribed rest—and a tablespoon of gin every two hours for relief of pain. This presented a problem, because Grandma was a teetotaler. Not wishing to offend her sensibilities, yet trying to make her well, Grandpa told her she was taking medicine that tasted bad. Trying to arrest her pain as fast as possible, he gave her a cupful.

Now, my grandparents lived next door to a small, neighborhood Protestant church. It was a Sunday morning. Soon parishioners began to arrive and settle in their pews, and the service began. No longer feeling pain, Grandma wished to share her newly found joy with others. She began to sing the old hymn "Bringing in the Sheaves." This, at the same time the minister next door mounted his pulpit to begin the sermon.

All the windows in both her house and the church were wide open on this sunny and hot morning. Grandma belted out her song contrapuntally to the minister's exegesis. As the pastor tried urgently to deliver his message, Grandma increased both the rhythm and volume of her own. It took many years for me to realize how much I admired and loved Grandma for her indomitable spirit.

Later, when I was in high school, I spent a summer with Grandma in the Midwest. I found her as bouyant as ever. A crisis occurred, however, when she discovered she had terminal cancer. She would handle this situation with the same resilience that she brought to everything else. There were no tears. Grandma set her affairs in order, swore me to secrecy about her condition, wrote a good-bye letter to my mother (to be opened after her death), and following unsuccessful surgery sailed off to heaven as if on a sea of blue.

My grandma remains one of the most arresting figures in my life. She was a great cook. I'll never forget her pot roast, vegetable soup, or lemon jelly cake. She was intensely human, a woman of emotion and passion, who learned that she must survive in what was then known as a man's world. She did.

My father was a powerful, albeit often negative, force in my life. Who was he? Why did he act in the ways that he did? When I could not understand him, was it possible to love him?

Observing my dad for the last time stretched out in a casket, I scarcely recognized him. His face was puffy and rouged. He was without the gigantic spark of life that had animated him in such a special way. Although I had often hated him, and feared my rage toward him might even destroy me, always I had found his humor a delight, his charm mythic.

Now, as a young priest, I read the burial office for my father, standing above his casket at the foot of the chancel inside a chapel. Later, in the cemetery, I committed his body, earth to earth, ashes to ashes, dust to dust. My father's body was placed beside that of his father, roots mysteriously mingled in the earth.

My dad was dapper, a great charmer, and a natural leader. Everybody seemed to like him, despite his drinking. I never felt close to him as a child. Our family was in a perpetual state of emotional chaos.

Dad was a man of enormous contradictions. An alcoholic with a legacy of two broken families (mine included) and several failed business enterprises, he finally quit drinking and turned into an amiable, wise, outgoing man with a caring third wife. So, while he had held success in his hand, lost it, stumbled, and struggled with self-destruction, finally he came to a happy ending. He beat all the odds.

His family's story was labyrinthine, fraught with violent change, rich in scandal. Ironically, Dad's father was an Episcopal priest in New York. An aged photograph of him, taken in 1890, shows him garbed in church vestments. It hangs on the wall of my office. Dad had a brother and three sisters, orphaned when both their mother and father died when they were young.

My dad was farmed out to live with an unspeakably rich and eccentric aunt who was rigidly set in her ways, holding absolute power over her limited world. When Dad ate at his aunt's table, a butler stood behind his chair. Dad had a natural rebellious streak, which was exacerbated by his discovery of the lack of freedom in his new domicile.

He ran away. Without any help from his aunt, he worked his way up from the bottom in the world of finance. Later, he and his brother, my uncle Reg, established their own firm. Reginald married great wealth; so did the three sisters. Happiness seemed to elude nearly everyone in the family, however. When Reginald died tragically young, his wife's Park Avenue suicide created tabloid headlines. Against the backdrop of a family destiny that in many ways resembled that of the larger-than-life family in the TV series *Dynasty*, Dad wed my mother following the breakdown of his first marriage.

Life was too fast in the roaring '20s, when the party never seemed to stop. In the absence of a real father, I was taught how to tie shoelaces and read the face of a clock by our family's chauffeur. Maybe Prohibition and speakeasies, bathtub gin and flappers created too hot an environment, for Dad had outrageous, risky affairs with women and drank with abandon. When Uncle Reg died, the whole house of cards came tumbling down.

Divorce followed in my family. My mother was given custody of me, and we moved away. When I was a boy, what I wanted desperately was to communicate with my dad. He had always seemed, even long before the divorce, to be half workaholic, half alcoholic. My family had never seemed to exist as a family, with my father, mother, and me playing roles in a strange charade. Memories of this time, and of my dad, are like theater scenes played behind a scrim.

The middle of the night. I have been sleeping for several hours. Now I awaken to the sound of glass breaking in the next room. I surmise my mother has hurled a glass-framed photograph of my father onto the wooden floor. I hear both their voices raised in anger and recrimination. He is shouting (he's drunk again), she is crying. He stalks out as a door slams. Silence. An ugly, scary, loud, terrifying silence. I want to run into the next room to hold and be held, cry out my feelings, find some plausible path. I lie in my bed alone, constricted, scarcely able to breathe, wanting to scream, feeling absolutely alone in both my room and the universe, wishing I could mercifully have oblivion.

Shift scene: Riding on a highway in an open convertible with my father and two of his business associates. All wear suits. He is drunk. They think the cold, rushing air will sober him up. Dad wears a Brando-as-Godfather visage. He does not say anything. Stoically he looks neither right nor left. The guys tell a joke or two, accelerating the car's speed;

we are careening like mad clowns down the highway. I can't relate at all to the guys, one of whom occasionally pats my head as if I were a dog.

Shift scene: In the house where I live with my mother after her divorce from my dad, it is an afternoon after school. The mail has arrived. There is a letter from my father. I feel that it is the golden grail. Communication! From my dad! It is real, I can hold it. I find a quiet place. I open the letter. "Dear Son." (He never wrote "Dear Malcolm.") He explains that he is having a hard time, but things are looking up; he expects me to be a good boy, have courage, help and support my mother, do well in school, and remember always that he loves me. He encloses a ten-dollar bill. He says nothing of the possibility of my visiting him or his visiting me. I am in limbo with a strange, distant father whom I do not really know, who lives half the country away. Why doesn't he seem to miss me? I do not know what to do. How to react to such a letter? I put on a diffident mask and try to act cool.

Shift scene: It is a week before Christmas. A big box has arrived addressed to me from my father. My Christmas present! All past bitterness and pain are forgotten. I clutch the box to my breast and carry it to my room. My father loves me. He is telling me so with the gift he has sent me.

I tear it open, paper scattered, strands of string askew. All of a sudden everything is macabre, noir, very bad. Inside the box is a suit of clothes that is not my size. If it were, I would not be caught dead in it.

It has no style, the color is wrong. I feel my dad has hit me with a solid blow. There is also a book inside the box. I love books, read them all the time, bring back a half-dozen from the library every Saturday.

But *this* book is one I would never read. Doesn't my dad *know* me? know what I would want to read? know what I would want to wear? I throw the box against the wall of my room, stomp on the suit, hurl the book, and shout in rage. How he could be so careless not to know me, *not to know me, not to know me, never to know me.*

Accepting my own humanity helped me, at last, to accept my father's.

I realized, finally, that he was no more a god or a devil than anyone else. He had managed to do battle nobly with his alcoholism and won (not taken a drink in thirty years). He sustained a good final marriage. People liked him. And I learned to. He became mellow, mature, seasoned, good-natured, sorrowful for wrongs he had committed (and, I think, acutely aware of them). A fondness and warmth developed between us. At this stage of my life, as I write this, I feel not the least touch of bitterness or rage. Forgiveness is something long in the past.

One thing that ultimately helped me to forgive my father was to shift my focus away from him to my own life—and get on with the living of it.

For many years my mother, Beatrice, lived in her own home, where she had a lemon tree, a rose garden, a pool in which she swam daily, and two dogs whom she loved. She was happy there until she fell and broke her hip. After that it became necessary to

My mother was known as a great beauty. She also possessed the attributes of a great lady: an awareness of the needs of others, genuineness, a natural simplicity, and qualities that received respect from virtually everyone.

spend the rest of her life in an institution that provided regular care.

When she was twenty, Beatrice volunteered to nurse and teach Navajo Indian children on a reservation in Arizona during the deadly influenza epidemic of 1918. An openness to the needs of others seemed to be a thread running through her entire life. At fifty-two, she began years of service as a parish secretary of an Episcopal church. Hearing informal confessions in the guise of helpful listening, and providing a structure of community of which she was a willing central figure, Beatrice became a forerunner of many women who, in a following generation, became Episcopal priests and bishops.

At seventy, after Mother retired, she began nearly two decades as a volunteer teacher at the Children's Hospital of Los Angeles. At this time, editor Ruth Nicastro of the diocesan *Episcopal News* called her "a role model for a new age."

Years passed when I took my mother's good health and sense of security for granted. How was I to know that a sudden crisis would shatter this condition of well-being? After an ambulance came to her house and attendants carried Beatrice away on a gurney, it became evident that she would never see her house again.

Her welfare suddenly became my responsibility. I had to learn quickly about such things as nursing homes, long-range care, and how to minister to her varied needs. Additionally, it became necessary to empty my mother's house, since she would not return there. The task of slowly looking through all my mother's possessions, handling them, thinking about them and their past associations, then making a final judgment about what to do with them, became a formidable and overwhelming task.

Here, before my eyes and at my fingertips, was the residue of someone's entire life, the record of a human existence.

Who could say what was important, what was not? I realize that many others have faced, or will face, the identical situation of dealing with a loved one's lifetime accumulation of possessions. This is a task that may, without warning, await anyone who is an offspring. A woman or man of fifty, with a parent who is seventy or eighty, needs a sudden surge of wisdom and energy, patience and maturity.

As I tried to sort through my mother's things, at times I laid my body on a couch, or sat down in a chair, mustering strength to complete an arduous task. I opened all of Beatrice's drawers and closets. I examined the contents of shelves, nooks, and crannies. Her dresser drawers were filled with underwear, stockings, and nightgowns. In closets were dresses, suits, coats, hats, and shoes. In the kitchen were dishes, silverware, pots and pans, canned goods, and a great iron kettle that had belonged to my grandmother.

On the walls hung oil paintings that my mother had done. I brought home a favorite of mine, one of lilacs in a vase. Her glass menagerie—a shelf of small objects, some glass, many prizes, souvenirs, and gifts—was much harder to deal with. Each object seemed to tell its own story, or was somehow a part of her story. I had to pick and choose.

I came across my mother's prayer book, *A Diary of Private Prayer,* by John Baillie, on a night table by her bed. I had given it to her many years before. It contained a month's prayers for morning and evening. She had prayed daily with this book for forty years. Its spine was broken, its pages falling out. Beatrice had jotted down her own notes on various pages.

Then I found a diary of her own, with "1948" embossed on its cover. She included a poem by Phyllis McGinley:

> Mothers are the hardest to forgive
>   Life is the fruit they want to hand you
> Ripe on a plate, and while you live
>   Relentlessly, they understand you.

Her final entry in the diary was her adaptation of some lines of Elizabeth Ackers: "Backward, turn backward, O Time, in your flight. / It has made me a child again—just for tonight."

What could I make of all this? (How is a child to know a parent?) Did my intimacy with Beatrice's significant possessions enable me to know her better, understand her more clearly?

Beatrice, my mother, handled old age with unerring grace, deep faith, and great reserves of inner strength. Here she is past the age of ninety. I had to learn fast about health care and nursing homes in order to care for her after she fell and broke her hip.

Always I found her indomitable. I admired her immense courage, incredible self-discipline, and desire to meet needs of others. Yet I wish that, following her divorce, she could have found a deep, emotionally rewarding relationship. I know she suffered periods of terrible loneliness for many years, which led to serious bouts of depression.

At the end of her life, she had virtually no possessions. In a drawer next to her bed in the nursing home were a hairbrush, a prayer book (that she could no longer read), and a tiny miniature of a dog that resembled her favorite golden Lab. On a corkboard placed on the wall near the foot of her bed were several photographs, along with a painting of Texas bluebonnet flowers she had done in 1934.

Her room looked out on a garden. She admired trees and watched birds. I was grateful for this, because she had been an artist when she was young and appreciated beauty. When I visited my mother in the nursing home it was hard to engage in a conversation because she was nearly deaf. So I resorted a lot to nonverbal communication. I made a point of looking directly into her eyes, gesturing, smiling, and laughing.

It was important to stay close and have physical contact. I tried to visit when lunch was served on a tray in her room. She liked me to share her food. Taking a spoon from her tray, I would help myself to a bite of salad or macaroni, green beans or custard. Beatrice laughed easily and thoroughly enjoyed this participation in her meal. Toward the end of her life, however, she ate less and less. There was an impediment in her throat and surgery was not considered advisable at ninety-eight.

Our visit always ended with saying the Lord's Prayer together. The traditional form—using "trespasses" instead of "sins"—was a vestigial part of her memory and very nature. After the prayer I would sit quietly with her, holding her hands in mine. Often during this time she would close her eyes or else look out at the garden. Before leaving, I embraced her for a few moments, holding her body close to mine. This essential physical communication bonded us close in spirit.

More and more people, growing older while having parents who are still older, will share the experience I had with my mother. Don't fight against it. Accept it. Treat it with mellowness, humor, charm, grace—anything you can muster. Be vigilant for a parent's rights in a nursing home. Visit regularly. Get to know the staff. Don't pull rank or get angry, but quietly and firmly make known your wishes and express your feelings in an easy way that is not threatening or abusive. If you play the prima donna or blustery CEO type and throw your weight around, it will accomplish less than nothing when you have left the premises and your parent or loved one remains there alone without you.

Anyone thirty, forty, or fifty may have occasion to visit people in a nursing home or convalescent hospital. Bring them flowers or a gift. Talk to them. Listen to them. Volunteer some time and service. Get used to this environment. Don't be a stranger to it. This will help if you have a parent or loved one in a similar situation. Who knows? You may be in a situation and a place exactly like this yourself some-day. Why not find out what it's like? learn the ropes?

Sharing my mother's experience has taught me a great deal. I realize now, more than I did before, that I shall take nothing with me when I depart Earth.

Yet I suppose friends of mine will inevitably search through what I leave behind, myriad objects I have accumulated, presumably trying to ascertain what personal meanings they held for me. This may help them to dispose of the objects responsibly.

Before inviting an AIDS agency to come into my mother's house and take everything that remained—from furniture to kitchen items, pairs of shoes to shelves of books—I placed special items of Beatrice's belongings in a small box. I included her wedding ring; a small gold watch; a Red Cross button from World War I; a small leather book filled with telephone numbers; three hand-painted scarves; the last letter her mother wrote her; her birth certificate (January 21, 1898); a snapshot of Beatrice as a girl—wearing black stockings, a fresh ribbon in her hair—posing with her puppy; and a U.S. Public Health certificate "given as an expression of appreciation for patriotic service voluntarily rendered" in the influenza epidemic of 1918–19.

This raises the question; What will become of my most treasured and intimate objects?

For example, there is Hippocampus Hudsonius. This seahorse, given to me when I was a small boy, came from the old New York Aquarium in Battery Park at the foot of Manhattan. Any outsider could not possibly know that Hippocampus Hudsonius is my oldest lifelong companion. Is it possible he could cavalierly be tossed away—unrecognized as an intimate of mine?

There are other objects close to me: an icon of Mary and Jesus, carved in ivory, that I brought back from Mount Athos, Greece, in 1955; a pair of opera glasses that belonged to my parents; a detail from the unicorn tapestry at the Cloisters in New York, a favorite place of mine; a miniature gondola from Venice, which I found on my first visit there; a small pottery vase, with green and blue flowers painted on it, from Crete; and two pieces of pottery—one black, one white—from the Taizé Community in rural France, where I lived and worked in 1957.

Harder to find, or recognize, is a flamenco evening program from Corral de la Moreria in Madrid. It is hidden in a stack of my handkerchiefs in a bedroom drawer. Inside the program, written in ink in 1961, are these words: "I hope you will always remember your first Flamenco night in Madrid." Why did I save and cherish this faded program? Because it reminds me when I was caught up in love in a passionate and unforgettable way. Very likely, this program would be thrown out with a stack of old magazines.Who could know its value and meaning to me?

All of us have our lovely secrets, our cherished memories. They remain largely unknown to others. I had no way to know Beatrice's secrets and memories. (Or my father's, or my grandfathers', or my grandmothers'.) After I am gone, who may briefly search through my few possessions and beloved objects, looking for meanings to explain my character and motivations, likes and dreams? I think it would be quite ironic if someone very sincere should unearth my entire truth, whatever that may be, and never know it.

I think there is a significant truth here. *As we live,* we should create splendid memories. Honor and savor them. Remembering is holy ground.

Chapter Three

SIMPLIFYING

In the night we were entertained by the sound of raindrops on the cedar splints which covered the roof, and awaked the next morning with a drop or two in our eyes.
— Henry David Thoreau

Autumn came overnight. The weather is colder, sharper. I need another blanket on the bed. I can no longer go barefoot on the patio or in the garden. The mood has changed. There is a fresh clarity and alertness, a moment of anticipation and quite different energy.

Watering the garden early in the morning, I discover the first lemons on a lemon tree planted several months ago. I drag the hose across the yard to reach camellias planted near a stone Buddha. I water the rosemary, irises, hibiscus, and on the patio, the fuschia and sword fern.

The anchor of the house is the pine tree. I find it serene, a steady friend and a dependable soul mate. Beyond a doubt, it will outlive me. I am always aware of its presence, its arms outstretched above the house bringing a sense of order and peace.

I take an early morning hike several days a week. It offers me solitude, the brilliant beauty of nature, mental stimulation, body awakening, and peace of soul. This morning a mist is palpable; I watch it move up a hill, cross a road. I am reminded of a poem I wrote in junior high school about seeing ghosts of Indian braves in a morning fog. On my hike today, people passing me on the path resemble figures in a medieval Chinese watercolor depicting a country scene. I feel a sense of detachment; the outside world is far away. The only sounds I hear are my footsteps on the dirt path, a bird singing in the distance, and faraway muted voices. I experience a sense of inhabiting eternity.

I like the challenge of my hike. I used to think I would never be able to reach the top of a towering hill. So I did not try. Then it occurred to me I might make it, so I tried. Now I navigate it easily. Yet when I look up all the way—the ribbonlike path a metaphor for my life's journey—it seems formidable. I keep going, my eyes taking in the pattern of other people's footprints in the dust. The next thing I know, I am nearly at the top. Then I am there.

I look out over the whole of the city. Even when my knees or hip are in considerable arthritic pain, I forget about this momentarily as I focus on trees surrounding me, foliage ringing my path, and people whom I encounter. I relate instantly to these fellow pilgrims. They *want* to be here; so do I. We connect by means of our mutual intention. I like these people, feel completely safe with them, and sometimes even spin stories in my head about some of them: a friendly elderly Japanese American couple, a young African American athlete who runs all the way up the hill, a middle-aged white woman listening to her Walkman.

During one of my hikes a man runs by, shouting, "There's a snake up there!" Rattlesnakes like this place. I used to be afraid of them. Now I've learned they have the same territorial rights I do. I just wait until they slowly cross the path before me, then I continue on my way. I also run into coyotes and wild dogs on occasion. We all keep going, minding our own business.

A hike like this clears my head, erases aches and pains, lends vitality to my spirit. I am sorry for people who never do this. At times I push ever farther, progressing around the next bend in the road, finally reaching another top of yet another hill. This is exhilarating beyond measure, until I realize I have a much longer return trip ahead. I do not venture farther today, run into coyotes, or see rattlesnakes.

Meeting humans is different. Many offer a greeting when we meet on the path. Ninety percent of the time it's "Good morning." Ten percent say, "Hello." Nobody ever says, "Hi." Teenagers tend to smile and make a point to be friendly. Some older people will wave a hand. I find it symbolic. A greeting, verbal or nonverbal, seems an acknowledgment that the walk up the hill is communal as well as an individual act.

I live in a house on a hill overlooking a busy street in Los Angeles that is usually filled by a rapid stream of cars. The home itself is a kind of miracle, a sanctuary hidden from the street by trees and shrubbery, nestled alongside a lovely, quiet garden.

After serving more than forty years as an Episcopal priest, it became necessary because of age requirements for me to retire from my ministry at the exciting and deeply spiritual parish of St. Augustine by-the-Sea in Santa Monica. However, I go on working unofficially. Five days a week I drive to the Cathedral Center of St. Paul, overlooking Echo Park Lake, not far from the hub of downtown Los Angeles, where I am poet/writer-in-residence, occupy an office, play a mentoring role, and function within a community.

This is in many ways the best part of my life. At certain moments I wonder whether I am a wary lion in winter or an energized teddy bear possessed of a soul. I realize that I am neither. I am me.

This morning I awaken ever so slowly, in childlike delight. My body twists casually in bed as a happy bear's might do in a cave. I do not move for a long time because I fear breaking the magic spell. I feel so deliriously happy and innocent, without a care in the world. Glancing at the clock, I notice it is still early. The alarm will not sound for another forty minutes. I feel bliss. This time is my total possession. I am perfectly content.

I am discovering that the child within me wants to play more than he used to. For example, there is my relationship with my car. I had an alarm system installed in it. When I get out of the car, I push a button on the key ring, which locks the car. Then it makes an abrupt sound, a kind of beep.

This, however, is followed by a second beep after I have taken a few steps away from the car. I have come to recognize it as a vulnerable cry of fright or insecurity. The car, as if it were my dog or cat, must wonder when, and if, I will return. It will be all alone until I do.

The other day I had parked in the garage at the Cathedral Center, locked the car, heard the good-bye beep, and to my surprise, called back to the car: "I'll be back. Everything's OK. You be good." At the same moment an elevator door opened and a stranger walked out. Taking in the scene, he backed off quickly and raced for his car. Did he feel I was over the edge? a wild eccentric? He didn't seem to understand that the child in me had spoken.

> When I am an old woman I shall wear purple
> . . . .
> And I shall spend my pension on brandy and summer gloves.

I like these lines from Jenny Joseph's poem "Warning" in the book *When I Am an Old Woman I Shall Wear Purple*. They are freeing. The poem signals independence. The message is: Go for it. Time is running out like sand in an hourglass. Do it now if you are going to do it at all. Tell someone, "I love you." Forgive that old hurt. Take that trip you are longing for. Dance that dance, write that book, buy those "summer gloves."

Age is not the issue; attitude is. These are freeing lines for everyone.

Poet T. S. Eliot offers in "The Love Song of J. Alfred

Prufrock" this possibility of a change in attitude. When I grow old, he says,

> I shall wear the bottoms of my trousers rolled
> . . . .
> I shall wear white flannel trousers and walk
>   upon the beach.

Taking a cue from Prufrock—though bypassing white flannel trousers—I visit a men's clothing store to shop. The young clerk, in his twenties, reminds me of myself when, as a college student, I worked weekends in a men's store. He shows me corduroy pants in four colors: gray, brown, pepper, and tan. I try them on. The tan makes me look like movie star Dick Powell in a musical or Alan Ladd in a film noir. It is out of character for me. The pepper is too somber, too dark. But the gray looks smashing. (The clerk tells me it will be very "in" this year.) The brown is nice because I look good in earth colors. I buy the two pairs.

Numerous times I've been told, "You can't be in your seventies! You look fifteen years younger." Well, I don't. But more to the point: Why should I? Is there something wrong with being my actual age? I suppose someone who is sixteen could ask the same question.

It reminds me a bit of the classic euphemism of the '60s, which has a white person address an African American using these words: "If all Negroes were like you, Bill, there'd be no problem."

Aging, like race relations and multiculturalism, gives rise to every kind of reaction, much of it insincere, hypocritical rubbish that masks the truth. But occasionally the truth appears in all its raw nakedness. For example, I was on the dance floor of a San Francisco disco one night, kicking up a storm, when a woman who was drunk addressed me in a loud, belligerent voice: "What the hell are you doing here, Grandpa?"

Bingo. No hypocrisy there. She was not what you would call polite, but she was certainly truthful—from her perspective. Yet if we're going to engage stereotypes when it comes to living, any of us may end up as a victim. One critic can adhere to a stereotype when saying, "For someone twenty I find you disgusting," while another may decry another's behavior with, "Acting the way you do at fifty is a disgrace."

Author Quentin Crisp noted: "The joy of being older is that in one's life one can, toward the end of the run, over-act appallingly." Yet why limit it to being older? Overact at twenty-five if you feel like it, or at fifty if you wish.

Individuality, including eccentricity, ought to be an option for anyone. There is entirely too much standardized, homogenized, socially prescribed behavior at all levels of our culture. When I was a kid, the classic movie *Frankenstein* was playing in theaters. I was turned off by the idea of a monster running amok, acting irrationally, terrifying people, and creating havoc. My worst nightmare would have been to run into Frankenstein on a forbidding country lane on a dark, rainy night. What if he'd been accompanied by the Hound of the Baskervilles, the Man in the Iron Mask, or the Bride of Frankenstein?

A half century later, however, I rented the video and watched the film at home. Quickly, I grasped that the demonized creature was not so much a monster as a victim. Frankenstein, who had never asked to be created, yearned to be loved, but was demonized as a stereotype lurking in people's imaginations. I realize now to what an extent most of us are conditioned by forces—ranging from entrenched attitudes to mass media images—that cause us to look at fabricated stereotypes instead of real people.

Simplifying, in my view, is knocking off stereotypes and (1) trying to be oneself while (2) permitting (or helping) others to be themselves too.

When one speaks of simplifying, a natural reaction is to conjure up a picture of letting go. There is a seductive element here. Wouldn't it be pleasant just to enjoy life more, simply relax, smell the roses?

Nearly twenty years ago I flew to Austin, Texas, to interview the extraordinary Barbara Jordan, the pioneering African American political leader and teacher, for a national magazine. Her grit and eloquence made her one of America's truly great women, and I loved meeting her.

After the story appeared, I began looking around for another exemplary person to interview. A celebrated actress-activist came to mind. But when I telephoned her public relations office to arrange an interview, I was somewhat dismayed and certainly disappointed when her publicist told me, "She doesn't have to do that anymore." My project disappeared on the cutting room floor.

Years passed. At a particular moment I felt bowed down by an overload of stress and pressure, because

I had overcommitted myself. The telephone rang. Here was a new invitation. I declined. Yet I was surprised to find myself thinking or saying to myself, "I don't have to do that anymore."

I felt guilty. Was I being selfish? Then I decided I was being sensible, doing the right thing. Had the time come for me to get out of the way? I could remove myself from a bright spotlight, make room for someone else—perhaps a younger man or woman. Why should I hog the act?

A lot of soul-searching followed. Finally, I decided that my response to this dilemma should not be characterized as either/or. I preferred both . . . and. In other words, I would neither walk away (give up responsibility, perhaps even act selfishly) nor would I try to accept everything, aggressively stay in the fast lane, and be all things to all people.

I could be selective, achieve a needed balance, continue to be of service, and search for purpose and meaning in each new day. I think that simplifying can mean shuffling a new deck, writing a half-dozen letters of resignation, slowing down (even accepting the fact that one is not indispensable), and looking intentionally in new directions.

Another useful way to simplify one's life is to relinquish harsh judgments, along with rigid, unyielding points of view. Let me share a personal story with you. For many years I reviewed both books and films for a variety of publications. My work had a sharp edge, and I took pride in that. Certainly I looked for flaws instead of strengths. (Here, my mentors were famed critics who did the same.) I believed that I was not a compromiser or someone with a soft side, and

I let the fur fly when I thought it should. I tried to be honest. In the process I hurt people's feelings, and from time to time gave rise to anger.

I suppose that I am mellowing now. I am more aware of the effort that goes into the creation of a work. It can require years and be horrendous in the price it exacts from a human being. It is easy for some idiot (perhaps myself) to be a snob, take easy pot-shots, look down his or her nose, and be needlessly subjective instead of objective.

I used to make up my mind fairly early in reading a book whether or not I liked it. Now I have learned to let that go, am content to wade through many pages without making a judgment, and often find hidden riches up the road. Presently I am reviewing a book. While commendable in a number of ways, I feel it needs to be more selective. (*Why* must it include the proverbial kitchen sink?) But along the way I've come upon fresh touches, welcome surprises, and good prose. It is a useful book that can speak to a lot of people. The author is lucky that I did not review it years ago when I was an enfant terrible.

More to the point, I'm glad that I am no longer confined to the rigid limitations of that role. I have been liberated in other simplifying ways, too. I can be myself, hold my views, make decisions without seeking shallow acceptance or obvious kudos from others, and be motivated primarily by the question: What needs to be done?

All of us share the task of striving to gather fragments of our lives into a pattern of wholeness.

A highly rewarding aspect of my being a mentor is to act as a spiritual advisor to a number of men and women, several considerably younger than me. It is my privilege to become familiar with their problems and dilemmas, yearnings and challenges, and to offer counsel. I listen closely, strive to understand, and point the way toward a clearer focus.

In the process of simplifying, spiritual centering and grounding become essential. An exterior life needs to be informed and sustained by an interior one.

Between my fingers a dead leaf on a weathered branch of a tree feels like crisp parchment. The wind blows steadily on this April afternoon as I wander through a cemetery located on a hilltop, isolated from mundane human activity.

A tombstone announces:

JOHN G 1829–1862

HIS WIFE
JUDITH ANN 1835–1909

DAUGHTER
NANCY MARGARET 1859–1937

An immense monument contains a single name, Esher, and a gigantic cross. Two orange flowerpots, one empty, the other half-filled with dirt, are overturned beneath in the dancing shadows of moving paper leaves.

In the distance a small green pine indicates visible life. An American flag waves in the breeze to the left, in front of a headstone. A wreath of dead flowers with a large, dirty red bow marks a tomb directly in front of me.

WIFE OF THOMAS PHIPPS

DIED 1893

AGED

48 YRS. 6 MO.

REST IN PEACE

An angel, a baby figure with immense wings carved out of stone, blows a trumpet over a grave to my left. A small bird flies over me through gaunt branches.

MOTHER

CAROL

A sacrificial lamb is carved atop a tombstone that bears the name Lucia. A wooden, suffering, thorn-crowned Christ, surrounded by small pine trees, is crucified over another tombstone nearby.

MY-SELF

proclaims one small tombstone. Sunlight catches the surface of a distant stone, making it shine like a windowpane.

Ashes to ashes, dust to dust. Here, a six-year-old boy lies buried. A tiny cement angel bearing a cross guards him. There a

NATIVE OF IRELAND

rests beneath the ground.

I wonder: Does passion lurk in dust? I rest here for a few moments, catching my breath, reflecting on my surroundings. I am grateful for this quiet peace, its lean simplicity, and yes, to be alive.

Chapter Four

MATURING

If you follow your bliss, you put yourself on a kind of track that has been there all the while, waiting for you, and the life that you ought to be living is the one you are living.

—Joseph Campbell

Some people place terrible limitations on themselves, which are, in essence, denials of life. These include chronic hopelessness, refusal to make a hard decision, remaining entrapped in a bad situation, resolutely holding on to a hard core of rage, withholding forgiveness, allowing tunnel vision to obscure a wide range of possibilities, and stubbornly maintaining a stance of rigidity, outlawing flexibility.

"I've come to realize a lot depends on our attitude," someone wrote me. "By its very nature our life changes constantly. We have the opportunity to change, grow, and discover new things and new aspects of ourselves. But it's necessary to open up, realistically assess what we have left (and where we want to go), and rely on our support systems to get us there."

I find decades are remarkable markers of our lives.

At thirty, I found myself caught up in radical change. The search for meaning was far more important to me than security.

At forty, my life was opening up far more than I had ever thought it could.

At fifty, much to my surprise, I was about to confront one of the major turning points of my entire life. I felt time was drawing near for me to focus on my inner journey. While in the past I had given a priority to my outer and public life, a big change seemed to be in order. The work of maturing beckoned in deeper ways.

God's role has been major in the long, arduous process of my maturing.

In my teens there loomed an angry God who, I felt, frowned on my occasional playful shoplifting to alleviate boredom and my frantic sometime cheating while sweating through a rough exam. This deity appeared to be judgmental, intent on letter-of-the-law scrupulosity, and a toss-up between a volcano about to go off and Bette Davis exploding in *The Little Foxes*.

In early adulthood, God the Grandfather emerged just when I needed him, with a voice like Lionel Barrymore's, solicitous, understanding, always readier to forgive than to criticize, and clearly possessed of unfathomable wisdom.

Decades passed before God the Mother appeared. It happened during the feminist movement. God the Mother seemed to be a cross between Eleanor Roosevelt and Marian Anderson, Georgia O'Keeffe, and Barbara Jordan. God the Mother was tough, a survivor bearing the weight of the human family on her back, who, despite having experienced every form of adversity, nonetheless retained a tenderness and vulnerability. I was delighted when *Ms.* magazine invited me as a male to write a cover story titled "Who's Afraid of Women Priests?"

During my participation in the '60s in the civil rights and antiwar movements, I found God the Son in the guise of Jesus overturning the tables of the money changers in the Temple. He was passionate, prophetic, reminiscent of John the Baptist, calling everyone to stark justice, and an alien from respectability and the sweet life.

Always I knew the God of nature and the universe: everlasting, discernible in a mountain range or the vastness of sky or sea, distant but involved, serene, endless, timeless, overarching, the ultimate icon of permanence.

I was in for a tumultuous shock on the day a reporter for the *New York Herald Tribune* telephoned to say it had been announced that God was dead, and did I have a comment? I was speechless. The "God Is Dead" movement had just begun in all its media glitter and multilayered meanings.

I studied God in other religious traditions, including Judaism, Islam, and Buddhism. As a Christian, I experienced God in the wonder, mystery, nurturing, and close familiarity of the Holy Trinity.

But then, for anyone living in the latter part of the twentieth century, there were all those cinematic images of deity to add to utter cultural confusion. These ranged from Laurence Olivier as Zeus in *Clash of the Titans* to George Burns in *Oh, God!* The presence of God was all over the place: Marlene Dietrich bowing her head in prayer in *Shanghai Express*; Joan Crawford seeking God's solace in *Susan and God*; Spencer Tracy teaching Clark Gable how to pray in *San Francisco*; Karl Malden fighting on God's side for justice in *On the Waterfront*; Henry Fonda confessing to God in *War and Peace*; Vivien Leigh, standing in the ruins of Tara, declaring "As God is my witness, I will never go hungry again!"

The list continues with Bing Crosby and Barry Fitzgerald as servants of God, Scotch-drinking priests in *Going My Way*; Richard Burton, a defrocked alcoholic cleric, desperately seeking God and life's meaning in *The Night of the Iguana*. Ingrid Bergman, Deborah Kerr, Audrey Hepburn, and Whoopie Goldberg were among the actresses playing nuns; Frank Sinatra and Johnnie Ray joined the ranks portraying cinema priests. Susan Sarandon gave an Academy Award–winning performance as a nun in *Dead Man Walking*, a contemporary religious portrayal that was moving and honest. Although ours has been a secular age in many ways, God has been neither absent nor inconspicuous.

In my life with God, God is deeply personal. I spend time with God in prayer on a regular basis. I am with God *here* and *now*; I believe that I shall continue to be with God after my body is cremated and my soul moves into the next phase of my eternal life. I feel the compassionate, close companionship of Jesus Christ as savior *and* friend.

When it comes to public worship, I tend to find ecstasy in quiet. Kneeling on a cold stone floor has often meant being on holy ground, consumed by spiritual fire. I believe the experience of the numinous and holy mystery occurs in God's time, not our own. These can overlap, but we cannot arrogantly summon God's time with a snap of the fingers, a million-dollar budget, or all the canned charisma in the world. We do not control God's time, or God, in any way.

At fifty, I began to settle into my experience of faith in ways that would continue to remain with me. Following a church-involved childhood, I pulled away from faith while I was in college. I told everybody I was an atheist—and thought I was. I've since learned that an astonishing number of people have had a similar experience. But then, as I moved into young adulthood in my twenties, I started to search for the meaning of my existence. What was I here for? Wasn't there more to life than work, play, companionship, home, and a bank account?

I sought refuge in the psalms, as found in my *Book of Common Prayer*: "I love you, O LORD my strength, O LORD my stronghold, my crag, and my haven." "As the deer longs for the water-brooks, so longs my soul for you, O God." "How dear to me is your dwelling, O LORD of hosts! My soul has a desire and longing for the courts of the LORD; my heart and my flesh rejoice in the living God." "Lord, you have searched me out and known me; you know my sitting down and my rising up; you discern my thoughts from afar."

As my faith deepened, the meaning of the sacrifice of Jesus Christ became overwhelming to me in its utter depth, its seeming unparalleled stretch of love.

How might I possibly be worthy of it? The words of the hymn "Amazing Grace" reminded me, again and again, that it was a pure gift. "I once was lost but now am found, was blind but now I see."

My maturing process was under way.

One of the big questions for me has always been: Can I make peace in my daily life, where I regularly confront crises, anxieties, and stress? live happily, creatively, get along with others? pursue common goals, tame my ego, look at things as they are instead of how I might like them to be?

Life is all of a piece. Everything is inextricably connected. Each moment, decision, and human contact holds its own significance. There is sharp specificity. Love is found *here* and *there,* so are hate and indifference, utter selfishness and cruel violence.

In my search for inner quiet and clarity, I visit a park one morning, walk by its trees and flowers. Now, up a path covered by fallen leaves. Next, down an embankment into a meadow. I sit beside a moving stream of water. I begin to look inside myself. An oak tree, its branches stretching overhead, reminds me I am part of the universe. The tree seems very, very still. I ask: Can I be too?

Thoughts move in my head. I had not realized what an emotional frenzy I had placed myself in. I see that my aggressive agenda is unimportant in the full scheme of things. Maybe I can quit wanting to win the world! (Is it really necessary to play Alexander the Great?) Looking at myself with a new honesty, I feel the crudest hypocrite when I say that I yearn for simplicity and quietness, then obviously deny this when I needlessly complicate my life and add to its disorder.

What, I wonder, is my biggest problem? Could it be, finally and simply, a refusal to grow up? Given my age and maturity, however, this strikes me as very, very strange.

I visit a museum to see four paintings that purport to depict four basic stages of human life. So a panorama of aging awaits me. What will I think of the artist's conception?

> The first presents a peaceful scene: a baby's happy existence.
> The second shows a youth standing heroically in an idyllic setting.
> The third represents middle age as being caught in the rapids of a mighty river. It is a scene of anxiety, near chaos, being tested to the limit.
> The fourth shows an aged figure resting in a posture of peace and contentment.

I know in an instant that my view of life is a different one. In the first place, I disagree with the depiction of a baby's condition as so sweet and uncomplicated. Far too many babies are impoverished, sick, hungry, and victims of abuse and dysfunctional families. I feel it is a mistake to manufacture such a pretty fantasy.

Even worse, in my view, is the simplistic stance of youth in an idyllic pose. This, in an age of drugs, sexual license, classist denial of equal rights to a good education, unequal health care, and a culture of violence out of control. Innocence is in abeyance.

I agree with the artist's portrayal of middle age as

akin to being caught in a river's rapids. Anne Morrow Lindbergh wrote in *Gift from the Sea* that most people in middle age have attained, or ceased to struggle to attain, their place in the world. I think this is less and less true.

Depicting old age as sheer and utter peacefulness, as the artist did, is absurd and an outright denial of reality. Indeed, life under fire is far more the norm than this simulation of nirvana. Because of this, many middle-aged men and women must also deal with *their parents'* problems—especially as these parents live longer and longer—as well as their own.

Growing older is a scream. Please let me explain. I find a twofold meaning to this. First, the one in Edvard Munch's classic painting of a person standing on a bridge, letting out a scream of bewilderment, rage, frustration, wonderment, or prayer. Second, what we find in the crazy humor, maddening pain, transcendent moments, passion, and challenge of simply being alive.

This image of aging was presented by Daniel J. Levinson in *The Seasons of a Man's Life*: "The connotations of youth are vitality, growth, mastery, the heroic; whereas old age connotes vulnerability, withering, ending, the brink of nothingness." It seems to me every variation is visible in all the stages of life. A person may experience the brink of nothingness at twenty, or exhibit vitality, growth, and mastery at sixty. Astronaut-Senator John Glenn revisited space at seventy-seven.

I am fond of these words written by Dame Ethel Smyth about age and beauty: "People who have been much loved retain even in old age a radiating quality difficult to describe but unmistakable. Even a stone that has been blazed on all day by a southern sun will hold heat long after nightfall." Beauty possesses no limitations. Neither does character.

Designer Donna Karan ran a remarkable magazine ad showing an older woman whose time-worn face, weathered neck, and hair with strands of gray bore little resemblance to images of conventional glamour that one ordinarily associates with fashion. This woman's photograph was startling because its honest depiction of authentic beauty defied ordinarily accepted norms.

In my seventies I find myself in a mentoring role with a number of people in their thirties, forties, and fifties. I strive to be a responsible role model. This does not mean acting a role. It means being myself, remaining open to life and other people, accepting responsibility, and continuing to grow.

My bedroom is filled with photographs, paintings, and books. A shelf holds a small army of animals: stuffed teddy bears, a Yale bulldog, a panda, an elephant, and a colorful rhinoceros. (One cannot have too much protection.) Hanging on a wall is a cover of *Look* magazine (July 27, 1971) that I shared with James Michener, Margaret Mead, Bill Moyers, Joan Baez, Duke Ellington, Walter Cronkite, and others. Above our photos the caption reads: "Troubled? Tense? 16 Prominent Americans give you their personal key to PEACE OF MIND."

In 1971 I never dreamt I would grow old. The magazine cover arouses nostalgia, carries me back through the years. My photo shows me wearing a

JULY 27, 1971

Troubled? Tense?
16 prominent Americans give you their personal key to

PEACE OF MIND

35¢

At last—
A movie your
kids can see

What
happened to a
good cop?

Elton John, 24:
How to make
$15,000 per hour

The Look *cover.*

shirt with bright red stripes and looking startlingly
young. Now, as I write this, almost three decades
have passed.

Recently I had an experience that had less to do
with "peace of mind" than with discovering that life
is a scream. At its conclusion I found myself physi-
cally and emotionally tired. In fact, I was wiped out.

It happened over lunch. There were three of us—one friend in his thirties, another in his forties, and myself—at a table on a charming outdoor terrace overlooking hundreds of sailboats.

I was trying to tell a story. But in a surreal way no one seemed to be listening to me. I felt it resembled a bad scene in a bad movie. It seemed their eyes weren't looking into mine. Were my words lost in a deep well or else scattered to the winds? I am not accustomed to feeling an outcast. Usually people appear to enjoy me as well as my words. Had something gone terribly wrong? Had I suddenly ceased to be a viable member of the group? I felt that my story did not mean anything to them.

I became conscious of my age in a most negative, unpleasant, and threatening way. I felt terribly old, even ancient, and that I had changed into a stereotype. One of my friends, a thirty-two-year-old man, seemed literally to have tuned me out. This, despite his obvious kindness, warmth, and consideration.

Was I imagining all this? In pain and disorientation, I blurted out, "I'm trying to tell a story!" A guilty silence fell like a guillotine. Both men focused on me. I wondered, was I being intolerably persistent, imperious as a domesticated King Lear? Quickly I completed my story. The conversation continued as if nothing inadvertent had occurred. Had it? Finally, I tried to make up for my gaffe by being overly jovial, amusing, and easygoing, a combination of a grandpa and Santa Claus.

I was exhausted. I had allowed my imagination—combined with low energy and a stupid, totally absurd fear of being left out of the loop—to cause me pain. I took a deep breath, let the dark shadows go away, and concentrated on my friends. I chose to accept the gift of living in the moment. I reminded myself: Life is worthwhile! It's something we do with other people. And a gift we can offer others is an example of courage or a large dose of humor, and a sturdy belief in hope.

Friends, of whatever age, are mentors to *me*. They touch my heart and soul, lift me up when I am down, listen to me when no one else wants to, and act as change agents in my continuing development.

I came across these words while reading John O'Donohue's book *Anam Cara: A Book of Celtic Wisdom*: "A friend is a loved one who awakens your life in order to free the wild possibilities within you."

I recognize that I have loved certain friends more than I've liked them, while I like others more than I can say I love them. I am grateful to those friends who have freed wild possibilities within me, pointed me in new directions, literally compelled me to grow, apparently feeling my life held a deeper purpose when even I was unable to perceive it. Sometimes when they caused me pain in the process, I was not at all grateful. I am now.

I seem to have a really eclectic assortment of friends. One, at forty, is a producer of film documentaries. He collects art, but his prize possession is a pet Moluccan cockatoo named Luke Skywalker. Luke shares my friend's apartment and has two cages: The first can be rolled from room to room as his master desires. The second is so huge that it fills a single room; here, Luke can fly. Despite having a powerful

Norman Mailer served as president of PEN American Center in New York while I was president of PEN Center USA West in Los Angeles. We're with actress Shelley Winters at a literary cocktail party in Santa Monica. PEN is the international association of writers.

beak, Luke is gentle in disposition. My friend likes to engage him in a conspiratorial kind of whispering bird talk.

Another friend is a natural poet, a comic who is a mystic voyager in a strange land, and as spiritual (though this remains hidden) as a desert monk. Eccentric and independent at fifty-five, he would surely have been beheaded or placed on the rack if he had lived in the Middle Ages. He is fortunate that the authorities have not caught up with him yet.

A brilliant, outgoing executive, another of my closest friends is, at fifty-five, also a woman of uncommon and essentially quiet faith. She remains an enigma to many because she combines the highest level of sophistication with disarming simplicity. The intricacies of her personality are mirrored by an Australian tea tree, its branches tightly twisted and at the same time enveloped in a warm embrace, that dominates the patio of her home.

An old and cherished friend is a multifaceted man who holds a key academic post in a major university during his daytime hours, then (on his own time) paints memorable canvases, cooks gourmet meals, and writes. At sixty-one, he has a droll, irresistible sense of humor as well as deep layers of sadness.

A wife and mother, another friend for many years, is an energetic, funny, optimistic, resourceful woman who raises friendship to the highest level of accomplishment. Our first meeting, which took place when I was a guest fellow in Calhoun College at Yale, proved to be unpredictable and hilarious. She and her husband invited me to their home near New Haven, Connecticut, for dinner one wintry night. It was snowing slightly, but seemed to present no problem. During dinner, however, we realized a blizzard had struck. We were, in fact, snowed in. I slept there the next two nights while snow kept falling. There was no delivery in the mornings of either milk or the *Times*. We found a lamb bone and vegetables, and spent hours preparing a robust meal. On the third morning, after the sun appeared along with the *Times* and bottles of milk, I took my leave. Quite by accident, or perhaps nature's intervention, an enduring friendship had begun with R. W. B. and Nancy Lewis.

Friends are great mysteries to me, like weathered trees. I have had a few who left an indelible mark on my life, then simply vanished; one day they just weren't *there* anymore. A few left my life abruptly after a misunderstanding; I never saw them again. A scar remained as I healed. One is terribly vulnerable to a friend, and can be sorely wounded.

Referring to significant changes that took place in a particular friendship, Michael Cunningham wrote in *A Home at the End of the World*: "Over the years we'd lost our inevitability together; now we were like the relatives of two old friends who had died."

Other friends are perennials. They turn up seasonally, or every few years; the friendship continues as if it had never been interrupted. I have one friend who remains from our early childhood; we understand without having to use many words; explanations are unnecessary.

Do you have friends whom you try very hard not to hurt? You know their vulnerability so well, their soft spots and places of potential pain, and you want to protect them.

One close friend's wife of many years died, and I felt completely inadequate. I wanted to *do* something to assuage the pain, but seemed unable to come up with anything practical. All I could do was be present in a patient and loving way, do chores, answer questions.

I remember the first time I had a friend who was black. I felt we lived in such different worlds, separate universes. Friendship meant bridging differences, overcoming separation, deep within ourselves.

Anti-Semitism was rife in the high school I attended. I held my breath as I commenced a friendship with a Jewish student. Would I say the wrong thing? *How* different were Jews? How could *I* know? What would other people *say*?

In high school I was shy, bookish, introverted, withdrawn. I had few friends and spent much time alone. But then I met my first gay friend, although I did not understand what that meant at the time. She was a university student and a lesbian, drove a red convertible, was a startlingly free spirit in a highly controlled environment—and befriended me. She took me to the smartest place in town, where the most chic crowd gathered. We ate and talked. I couldn't get over the fact that she wasn't ashamed or embarrassed to be seen with me. I felt that I was nobody, unattractive, poorly dressed, and certainly devoid of fine conversational skills. But she drew these out of me with infinite charm and patience. Someone loved me, and let me know it. It was wonderful.

It is important when we are feeling low and a friend telephones and makes us laugh. It is a blessing to be able to break down and cry in front of a friend who shares the pain.

How grateful I am for a friend who tells me the truth when I don't want to hear it, letting me know I am wrong about something and need to change.

I suppose friends have influenced me most deeply by introducing me to alternative ways of thinking and feeling, and have shown me by their example how to risk taking an unknown path or to stand up for the cause of justice.

So, as I prepared to write this book, it was the most natural thing in the world for me to turn to a number of friends, asking for their help and contribution.

What, I asked them, did they feel about maturing, growing older, facing up to life, and finding meaning?

A man who is thirty-nine: "As I have started doing inner work with an analyst, I have explored some of the repressed, shadow parts of my unconscious and become much more at home with my aging. In fact, I have begun to appreciate my age because I see how much experience I have that many younger people don't have. I believe that I am a much more interesting and engaging person than when I was younger."

I know this man well. I appreciate his recognition that he is actively aging at thirty-nine. He offers much of his life to public service. He's intense, committed, often droll and funny, and mature beyond his age.

A woman who is fifty-one: "Usually when I wake up in the mornings I am amazed that I woke up at all. Often I find I had no awareness of being asleep. I've always had an active dream life. I am preoccupied with the past, because I'm angry about all my stolen and spoiled moments. My plans are unchanged because they've remained ill realized. My dreams have consumed me."

This African American woman has known the pain of struggling against oppressive forces and stereotypes that have stood in the way of her personal freedom and professional advancement. She possesses immense courage and energy, and refuses to sacrifice her dreams.

A man who is seventy-nine: "I like the lack of pressure, the freedom, without ambition gnawing at me. I like saying exactly what I think. I like seeing my grandchildren grow, and having some younger friends. But I miss the buoyancy of youth. No more really crazy times. Not as many laughs and wild parties, crazy trips, risky adventures. I don't think I am as creative as I was and I get a little more easily tired, but when I have enough sleep and the adrenaline rolls, I still have drive and, unfortunately, am still compulsive."

This man is famous. He has scored memorable successes and made major contributions to contemporary society. He still has great buoyancy. Never a hypocrite, he remains forthright, disarmingly honest, and a rebel with many causes.

A woman who is fifty-two: "Aging is on my mind. My father died six months ago at eighty. My father's sister is in the hospital for hip surgery. My mother's brother has Alzheimer's. Yesterday, at the age of seventy-eight, my mother went to the Marriage License Bureau and got a license for her second marriage. I've started going through menopause, and two weeks ago my son (who turned fifteen in March) got his learner's permit to drive a car. If I wanted to ignore the fact I'm aging, it would take a concerted—perhaps heroic—effort. My mother once told me that she was watching her mother grow old so she would know how when her time came."

This woman is a fine role model for her daughter. A lawyer, activist, and consummate volunteer in community organizations, she combines a healthy sense of humor with an obdurate determination. I have learned that when there is a need, she tends to be present as a friend.

A man who is sixty-seven: "I can see that acceptance of death involves a certain surrender of the self—of *selfishness*. And since I struggle a lot of the time with how self-centered and controlling I am, I think this may be of one piece. Selfishness equates to fear of death—and to clinging to control, which I like."

I am intrigued by the fact that this man, whom I admire, seems far less self-centered and controlling than he apparently believes he is. He is accessible to the needs of others, and while he's a strong, assertive leader, he is actually quite self-effacing. Or so it seems to me.

A woman who is forty-seven: "It's interesting how aging does not really have anything to do with maturity. My ten-year-old-daughter is more mature than many older people. Why do some people develop character, integrity, and compassion while others do not? Why do some people grow from experience and others do not?"

This remains a universal question. Logic and rationality do not seemingly help to answer it. As the sun rises and sets, so do people go their way— some growing from experience and blossoming, others not.

A man who is forty-one: "The thing about life is that, if you think about it, we're in the midst of dying

every moment. Every moment we're a new person—
new atoms, new thoughts. The 'me' of five minutes
ago is now dead; now I'm another 'me' who perpetu-
ates the sense of myself. This gift of consciousness is
terribly important to me right now."

I find this comment especially poignant because
this man recently had a mysterious, lingering illness
that seemed to threaten his life. He struggled with
the crisis valiantly, step by step, and grew spiritually
before my eyes.

A woman who is forty-seven: "Some of my closest
friends are seeing the aging process in their fifties as
pretty bleak. They see their professional opportunities becoming limited by their ages. They are pan-
icked about money. They are paranoid about their
health. They are too busy paying present debts to
fantasize about retirement. Some of them have
young children, no savings, and inadequate insur-
ance. My daughter, at eleven, is a source for me of
incredible vitality and an excuse to laugh, act silly,
and stay creative. I wonder how I will fare seven or
eight years from now when she leaves me to make
her own life."

These views do not come only from this woman's
friends, but from her own experience too. She feels
overwhelmed by a combination of approaching
problems. I appreciate her clarity and honesty.

A man who is seventy-two: "Sensuality? Two or
three times a week isn't enough? I love good dirty
movies and porno, and I love to look at a naked
woman. Call me pervert. Beautiful women are a work

of art. I expect to age well. I want to die at home in my bed, or in some woman's arms having sex, or just plain drop dead in the garden without crushing the plants."

It might surprise you, if you tend to see stereotypes in place of flesh-and-blood people, that this man is a well-known, distinguished religious leader. He has always had a strong passion for life.

A woman who is seventy-seven: "My body hurts, I grunt when I get up from a chair, I puff when I go uphill. I cannot work eight hours in the garden as I used to. But my mind is clear as crystal. I think better than I ever did. I have achieved a level of awareness when I can make connections and analyze as never before. What we have as aged people is a storehouse of information, feelings, experiences. We who have been blessed with the potential of a long life are excited to keep going to see what's next."

I know her well. Long ago she said good-bye to a husband who died, raised a family, undertook a demanding job of health service, and got involved in a number of controversial community issues. Not always a particularly easy person (especially if you are trying to manipulate her), nonetheless she is a somewhat saintly one.

A key part of maturing is understanding life better, acquiring experience and wisdom.

From a center of peace one can acquire a view of the world that possesses more love, humor, equanimity, and hope.

Always, time is running faster than an action film.

It is easy to become obsessed by this idea. So, it is altogether possible to start acting a bit like a maddened centipede lying on its back, its feet twisting aimlessly in the air.

The truth is: Always there is little time. So we must get on with the task of living. This requires maturing.

Chapter Five

EXPLORING

ake voyages, attempt them, there's nothing else.
—Tennessee Williams

think not only of the places I have been but also of the distances I have travelled within myself.
—Laurens Van der Post

Exploring is what life is all about. As all of us know, at the beginning we're simply here. It's all new, a complete mystery. Around us are people. Objects. Surroundings.

As we grow, we adapt to a series of realities. All the time, we're exploring: Here or there? How to do this? Why must we do that, and with whom?

Kindergarten is exploring. So is starting first grade, finishing college, innocently coming upon poetry, studying biology, hearing Mozart for the first time, taking that initial hike, immersing oneself in a pool of water and learning how to swim.

Exploring includes finding our way around a new school with unexpected companions and formidable-looking teachers, its classrooms and lockers; beginning to trust friends while getting used to the irksome task of getting along with enemies; colliding with clashing images of glamour, celebrity, success, and failure; growing into a sense of the faraway, immense world with all its diversity. Some learn to be at home with the embracing world; others shrink from its sheer size and awesome mystery. Archetypes of explorers have ranged from Ulysses to Marco Polo, Columbus to Amelia Earhart.

Of course, we are all explorers. Most of us (at least at times) yearn to delve into the unknown, scale a peak, move lightly twenty thousand leagues under the sea, be received elegantly by a distant potentate, unveil a hitherto impenetrable mystery, or dine on the world's finest menu.

The dictionary speaks of exploring as visiting a region, examining or studying, a search—for a river, a mountain, a desert, or peace of soul—and having discovery as its purpose.

I have engaged in numerous forms of exploration. You must have done so too.

On a desert shortly before sunrise, I climb down a hill and reach out to touch a worn, gnarled, and twisted plant that looks like driftwood. A gigantic rock, shaped like a stolid Goya figure, leans in my direction. When the sun bursts forth, I am caught in its fire. I am stunned by joy and gratitude.

Bright lights illuminate the ancient stones of the Western Wall in Jerusalem at midnight. Notes that people have written, many of them prayers, are lodged in holes in the rocks. I place my forehead against a rock in the wall and pray.

Visiting a lodge in a great forest, I look out on a vista that includes thousands and thousands of trees as far as my eye can see. I experience a remarkable moment of quiet and peace, and am amazed when the moment holds. I simply move in it and with it. As I gaze on the incredible firmament, giant formations of clouds engage in slow, easy motion. In my head I hear Bach. Motion and being are perfectly synchronized in highly complex action. There is clear intelligence, overarching spirit. All this is infinitely more than I can easily fathom. I just let it be, and let myself be.

Early morning mist closes around Mount Athos off the coast of Greece as our small open boat approaches, coming from the village of Ierissos. The boat holds a few people, a donkey, and sheep, their feet tied together. Later that afternoon I wander among stone ruins on a beach near the monastery of Vatopedi. Chimes peal inside the walls where I will spend the night. In a moment following sunset, when darkness is about to fall, I wait.

Hiking, I find myself in a deep valley between towering hills. I lie on the ground, wanting to be quiet and meditate. But I feel no peace or serenity here. They say this circular space was created eons ago by a falling meteor. I wonder if everyone who lived here was killed when the disaster occurred. There is no sound. Not a blade of grass moves. The scene seems frozen in time. Time is different here, if it is time at all. Yet it must be, for I am aware of it. Every second seems to hold the power of life or death. I know that I am on the edge of my own life. Only two of us are here: a great, incalculable power and me.

During the mornings I worked in the fields when I lived in the Taizé Community in rural France in 1957. At noon a bell rang, summoning everyone to noon prayers and lunch. A member of the community offered intercessions, often for people prominent in that day's news. For example, if I heard the names Eisenhower and Dulles, I knew instantly they had figured in some special way in that day's public events. The community subscribed to the newspaper *Le Monde*, so I could later read the paper to find out what had happened. I liked the cycle of this simpler, structured life: work, prayer, community. I tried to hold onto some of its elements when I returned to the U.S. and the hurly-burly, the stress and fast motion of my daily life.

I am an explorer, a sojourner. So are you. Always our outer journeys occur. Sometimes they are in sync with our inner journeys, other times, unfortunately, they are not. One of our most important life tasks, in my view, is to bring them together. When we can do this, we are no longer working at cross-purposes within our lives. So, we can cease making outer voyages in order to run away from our inner selves. Our lives become integrated. These inner journeys are inevitably our most significant ones.

I lived and worked in the French monastic community of Taizé in the 1950s. It was an experience that had a profound impact on the rest of my life. I returned to the United States and my first parish in Indianapolis in 1957.

Within my own
soul and mind
are many places
enigmatic and unknown

A towering peak of ego
unwalled city of vulnerability
quiet sanctuary of faith
vast desert of raging storms

Silent words speak to me
in a labyrinth or maze
by quicksand
in tumult

Have I loved the world enough?
too much?
have I loved others enough?
too little?

Instruct me
change my ways
penetrate my stubborn pride
warm my heart

Exploring means reaching out. There is a whole world out there.

Exploring means risking instead of dying prematurely.

Exploring means being adventuresome and celebrating life. Exploring means letting changes take place in our life, sometimes becoming an active agent of change instead of a passive onlooker.

"I'm looking at a solid brick wall," a sixty-five-year-old man told me. "This is very scary. Suddenly, I have no goals remaining. Realistically, are any new opportunities or options viable for me? I seem to have no itch for a new adventure, no clear purpose, no ambition. Is it over for me?"

This man, trying to make adjustments in a difficult time of transition, gives an appearance of being a prisoner locked inside a cell. Yet it's altogether possible the prisoner locked himself inside. He alone may hold a key to unlock the door. We should not place limitations on ourselves or on our very real possibilities. We are all going to die later; why not live now?

Even when I was a kid, life beckoned to me in an inviting, friendly way, despite adversity. I had enormous obstacles in my path, but I believed, and still do, in hard work, perseverance, occasional miracles (particularly if I do my own part in helping them along), and the reality of hope.

I have refused to give up, even when my circumstances provided a logical reason to do so. I kept reaching out—to life, other people, and possibilities—instead of closing down. I took breathtaking risks, both for myself and for other people.

A basic motivation of mine is that I believe in change as a natural part of living and as a quality of God's will. Life does not remain static; a part of our responsibility as human beings is to stay flexible and keep growing.

I was a rich kid who became poor after the money ran out. Lavishly spoiled and overprivileged as a youngster, I experienced hunger and deprivation as a teenager in the Depression. I had a job in the mail room of a medical supply firm during high school years, and I got my Social Security number. In college, I waited on tables (and washed the dishes) at a sorority three times a day, six days a week, and worked some evenings at a local radio station. I worked my butt off. And I found it an often funny and exciting adventure. While doing this, I also published a small, independent journal of campus news (and sold ads for it), at the same time working on the college newspaper, poetry magazine, and yearbook.

Coming to Hollywood, I was employed by the Foote, Cone & Belding advertising agency as a "junior executive" and given a daily fifteen-minute radio program to produce. After that came movie jobs and, at twenty-five, my business partnership with Mary Pickford.

I learned that working in Hollywood was a bit like being an actor in the movies themselves because, for

Edgar Bergen, one of the entertainment industry's most popular stars, made a guest appearance on Hollywood in Three Dimensions *on KTTV in Los Angeles. I emceed the show and coproduced it before departing Hollywood for seminary.*

the first time in my life, I found myself literally rubbing elbows with famous stars. I couldn't believe it. It was exhilarating to be on the same dance floor with a movie goddess, or have lunch in a booth next to Bing Crosby's, or attend a party where a dozen major stars chatted and relaxed.

A far more direct encounter was found by actually working with John Wayne, Dame Judith Anderson, Lillian Gish, Claudette Colbert, Maria Montez, Peter Lawford, Gloria Swanson, Paul Henreid, Robert Young, Cecil B. DeMille, Hoagy Carmichael, Roy Rogers, Dale Evans, and many others. I found out (usually the hard way) that movie gods and goddesses were controlling, difficult, insecure, and sometimes tortured human beings. Maybe it was even worse for them than the rest of us, because they were asked to wear tight masks, play the same roles, which never ended, and become inseparable from their public images.

A tragic figure was Charlie Chaplin. No one had been a bigger star, admired throughout the world. Then came acrimony and denunciation; adulation turned to disrespect, even hostility.

Charlie Chaplin Jr., his son, was a friend of mine. One New Year's Eve we went out on the town to celebrate at Ciro's and the Mocambo, two popular clubs. As Charlie drove his new Cadillac, a Christmas gift from his father, he collided with another car on the Sunset Strip. Police were on the scene immediately. It was only a minor traffic mishap, but when the press found out Chaplin's son was involved, it became a major cause célèbre. Huge, black headlines announced the news.

The next morning Charlie and I went together to visit his father in his Beverly Hills mansion. Mr. Chaplin was somber, caught between outrage and sadness. He knew that his son was the tragic victim of his father's celebrity, and there was little or nothing he could do to help him. Shortly afterward, Mr. Chaplin left the United States to live in Switzerland for many years. I knew a number of similar unhappy stories about people who were caught, often innocently or inadvertently, in the grinding machinery of image making. Careers careened when box office slipped; fame gave way to indifference; one's image—which had exacted sacrifice in terms of human worth—was found worthless.

Yet, I wouldn't have missed my Hollywood experience. The then-new TV industry was getting underway and I coproduced two early shows, hosting one of them. It was a heady time. I was president of the Television Producers Association of Hollywood and, in 1951, received an honorary Emmy—"in recognition of his distinguished and outstanding service"—from the Academy of Television Arts and Sciences.

Clearly, I liked to work. (Or, I liked *my* work. My advice to someone who does not is to get out and change one's type of work, if possible.) However, there was more to it than that. I found work provided me with a zest for life. Each day held its own high excitement and motivation. It still does.

When I entered a seminary to become an Episcopal priest, and after my ordination, I envisioned a quieter existence. I was wrong. A contemporary clergy life is anything but soft: a mix of spiritual leader,

Roy Rogers and Dale Evans were old friends, so it was good to see them when they visited me during seminary days in Berkeley at the Church Divinity School of the Pacific. They're with two of their children.

administrator, fund-raiser, community spokesperson, preacher, and counselor. I plunged into my pastoral tasks. Society, however, was changing radically and fast. So was the church.

Undoubtedly I was too idealistic about the church, even a perfectionist. When it showed obvious flaws, such as its maddening genuflection to racism, I reacted with outrage and anger. How dare the church not be Godlike? Too, flaws in professed Christians—such as careerism, egotism, signs of professional bureaucracy over against commitment to social justice—disturbed me.

Did I think I was better than those whom I criticized? No. I felt, in fact, inadequate and sinful, and
prayed that I might be used by God despite my failures. So I held myself up to the same impossible
standards that I imposed on everyone else.

As a result, I became a rebel. I criticized "churchianity," asking for a higher standard of commitment. I
rejected the ordinariness of human life, including my
own. Perhaps I was afraid of it, or did not know at
that time what to do with it. The fact that I was gay,
closeted, and hadn't a clue how to handle *that*, con-
tributed to my dilemma. I was extraordinarily sensi-
tive and vulnerable.

The way ahead was clearly set for a disaster course
(although I was completely ignorant of it) when, as
Episcopal chaplain at Colorado State University in
1959–61, I announced a series of "Expresso Night"
events. The phrase had cropped up in an English
film, *Expresso Bongo*. A student explained: "It captures
the feeling we have of wanting to express ourselves,
of needing a way of expression that is free and unin-
hibited." These evenings comprised folk songs, read-
ings, and dance. The *Rocky Mountain News* headlined
a story: "MINISTER SANCTIONS RELIGION
WITH A COOL BONGO BEAT."

The story went on to say:

> Flickering candlelight in a dim, smoke-filled
> room, the throbbing beat of bongo drums, the
> melancholy words of poets loved by the avant-
> garde set, the haunting rhythm of the blues. This
> is "expresso night" at St. Paul's House on the edge
> of the Colorado State University campus. It is the
> "out group" that Father Boyd is attempting to

reach, as well as serve the others through more ordinary church services. . . . "Christ came not to save the church but the world," is one of Father Boyd's favorite expressions and he puts it into practice by putting himself into some unorthodox situations where he is available for those needing help.

All hell broke loose when the bishop of the diocese, who never came to take a look at an Expresso Night for himself, attacked it and wrote: "You can't think of yourself as a beloved son of God and at the same time go around with matted hair, dirty bodies, and black underwear." (He was referring to beatniks and leotards.) "Heaven is your home," he continued. "Don't allow the puny minds of modern intellectuals to rob you of the great truths revealed to us by the Holy Spirit through the ages."

Of course I responded, so vigorously that I shook all the leaves off the tree. There was a national furor, a storm in a teacup. My departure was announced. Letters poured in. This was my favorite: "The Apostles must most certainly have smelled of fish, Job was at his best when sitting on a dung hill, and it is to be presumed that Stylites had no bathing facilities on top of that pillar. Our best Christians have been an odiferous and malcontented rabble, and you are to be congratulated for reminding us of that."

Although I was given a new job as Episcopal chaplain at Wayne State University in Detroit, my life had changed unalterably. I received a new identity in a *New York Times* headline: "BEATNIK PRIEST QUITS CHAPLAINCY."

In retrospect, it is funny. Then it was dead serious. Dubbed a barn burner, I guess I set out at least to be a good one. The *Washington Post* (February 6, 1965) wrote: "'Please don't call me controversial,' pleaded Malcolm Boyd, Episcopal minister, ex-atheist, ex-Hollywood television producer, freedom rider, playwright and twice-resigned college chaplain." The *London Evening Standard* (March 22, 1967) chimed in with: "Boyd is a full time disturber of the peace, a jarring blend of Luther and Lenny Bruce, who is attempting to shock religion into being relevant."

Good came out of all this when I embarked on a decade of very deep involvement in the civil rights movement, a significant turning point in my life that changed me forever, leading me into new ways of risk and service I had never dreamed of. At the same time, I learned firsthand how incredibly controversial religion can become when its quiet waters are stirred. I found numerous friends inside the church who shared the same thoughts and feelings. One was Bishop Paul Moore Jr., of New York, a mentor and friend.

Looking back, what did I learn and how was I changed?

I still object to plastic churchianity.

I still believe that Jesus—passionate, inclusive, unconditionally loving—would be rejected by many members of churches if he wandered in and walked up the center aisle on a Sunday morning.

I still believe the church, at its best, comforts the afflicted and afflicts the comfortable—or, at least, jabs their conscience and makes them sit up and take notice of glaring human needs.

So, you see, I *took* risks, actively worked for *change*, and quite intentionally pursued *exploring*. I strongly recommend these to someone at fifty or any age. There is no age limit.

Looking back over the seventy-seven years of my life, I see a long series of turning points. (I wonder what are the turning points in *your* life—those moments when you pursued *this* path over *that* path, staked out a whole new area of life, went exploring, and courageously opted for real changes.) It seems that I have always been on a very conscious journey, moving forward with a sense of adventure and what one might even call pilgrimage.

My first big turning point was the dramatic one of graduating from college and literally plunging into that magically strange world called Hollywood, seeking my fortune there with youthful abandon and ardor.

The second was leaving Hollywood and entering a seminary. I would say a third turning point was undertaking additional years of theological education and work that took me to England, France, Switzerland, and Germany and introduced me to such exciting new experiments as the "house church" and "industrial mission," as well as the challenge of the ecumenical movement. In other words, instead of settling into the parameters of a U.S. parish, I set out on an adventure (I had no map and didn't know my way at all) that changed the course of my life.

All these experiences combined to move me away from conventional religion in another turning point: To commit myself in the justice struggle of the civil rights movement. My involvement began in 1961 when I was invited to participate with an integrated group of African American and white Episcopal priests in a prayer pilgrimage/freedom ride in order to test segregation laws and protest apartheid. A decade of civil rights work followed. It involved voter registration of blacks who were disenfranchised as well as grassroots efforts of many kinds to achieve racial justice, increase understanding between people by confronting realities, and support racial integration instead of separation.

We found ourselves in a time that demanded strong individual conviction and solidarity with others equally gripped by conviction. When hypocrisy, double-standard morality, and legalistic maintenance of injustice prevailed, we felt protest was called for.

This proved to be the most intense, and often harrowing, period of my life. I had never thought I was courageous (or particularly needed to be), yet now I acquired courage as a means of human survival. I guess I was not unlike the cowardly lion journeying through Oz.

In 1962, I took part in a ten-hour sit-in at a segregated restaurant in Tennessee. After dark a flaming cross exploded on a lawn outside. An angry, drunken crowd threatened us. Several months later, I stood in the light of early morning on a quiet street in Jackson, Mississippi, and inspected the bullet hole in a window of the home of Medgar Wiley Evers, the NAACP leader who had been murdered two days earlier. Three hours later I crowded into a hot auditorium for his funeral. A minister repeated his widow's words a few hours following her husband's

I'm with other Episcopal priests standing beside an African American church that was bombed in McComb, Mississippi, during the civil rights struggle. We were horrified by what we saw and determined to change existing conditions if we could. Quinland Gordon is on my left, and Earl A. Neil is on my right.

death: "I wonder if he has died in vain?" Then the pastor told the mourners: "That question belongs to you today. It is for you to decide if he has died in vain or not."

Afterward, we moved outside the hall into the street for a funeral march. Thousands of us, blacks and whites, marched from the funeral to the funeral home. We were four abreast in a weaving, relentlessly purposeful line that stretched out behind almost as far as the eye could see. I shall never forget the dozens, or hundreds, of faces that I studied, as they also studied mine. Faces were profound, feelings behind them deep.

A mentor of mine during these years and experiences was Richard A. English, who is now dean of the School of Social Work at Howard University in Washington, D.C. His counsel and wisdom were often enablers of my activism. Two other people who became active persons in my life were Jonathan Daniels and Viola Liuzzo. They were martyrs of the civil rights movement, and I shall mourn them always.

On other occasions I carried a picket sign with the Rev. Henri A. Stines for hours outside the Lovett School in Atlanta when it rejected the application of Martin Luther King III and other young black students; stood on the steps of the Dearborn, Michigan, city hall—surrounded by egg-throwing, shouting hecklers—protesting the de facto system of all-white real estate; integrated (accompanied by another white man) a black motel in Natchez, Mississippi, as a half-dozen African American men and women simultaneously integrated two white motels; marched with Marlon Brando in a Los Angeles suburb to protest a segregated all-white housing tract; joined black students in Virginia to picket a movie theater in protest against a segregated seating policy; marched outside the Syracuse, New York, police department to protest alleged police brutality; worked in rural Mississippi and Alabama during the summer of 1965 with the Student Nonviolent Coordinating Committee on voter registration; picketed the City and County Building of Detroit to protest housing practices; and assisted (along with an

African American priest, the Rev. Quinland Gordon)
in the work of black voter registration in McComb,
Mississippi, where a black church had been bombed.

What did it all mean? For me, the main meaning
was people, created in the image of God, who were
dehumanized by tradition, but too often for demonic
reasons of hate and exploitation. Finally, in the spirit
of God's love, one must act for the sake of justice.
Soon, one learns that personal experience breeds
involvement.

> It is the summer of 1965
> in rural Mississippi
> driving at midnight
> I am the only white person
> in a car with African Americans
> we are civil rights workers
> a car looms behind us
> lights blinding
> who are they?
> the car abruptly speeds past
> vanishes in the darkness
> but at a fork in the road
> there it is again
> lights turned off
> waiting
> soon it follows us again
> on deserted dirt roads
> I have never felt more afraid
> what will happen?
> will we be all right?
> my chest hurts
> I pray

Following the freedom ride and other experiences,
I wanted to make a dramatic statement about human-

ness. At the same time, bail money was raised for arrests in connection with the freedom movement. As a result, I wrote a short one-act play called *Boy*. In its premiere performance in a Detroit coffeehouse theater I played the part of an African American shoeshine man, wearing a black mask. *Boy* was later performed on a tour of university campuses, in the National Cathedral in Washington, D.C., and in many parts of the U.S. The NBC television network showed excerpts from it. Then I wrote three more short plays contained in a trilogy: *Study in Color, They*

I am wearing a black mask and appearing in Study in Color, *one of the short plays I wrote about race. Actor Woodie King Jr., wearing a white mask, is with me in a Florida coffeehouse.*

Aren't Real to Me; and *The Job.* I told the *New York Times* the plays represented a frank attempt to disturb audiences and puncture smugness about human injustice.

To anyone younger who is reading this, let me say that I shall always view my participation in the civil rights movement of the '60s as the most deeply meaningful period of my life. The cause of justice must always take precedence over other matters, both public and private.

Still another major turning point of my life came, to my utter surprise, when a small book of prayers I had written, *Are You Running with Me, Jesus?* became a runaway bestseller in 1965. Poet Langston Hughes and many critics called the prayers simply "poems." The celebrity of the book, with all the excitement it generated, turned my life around in many unexpected ways. One million copies were in print. The signature prayer became well-known: "It's morning, Jesus. It's morning, and here's that light and sound all over again . . ."

The underlying point in my own life was that I was still taking risks, finding myself involved in fundamental changes, and discovering great adventure in exploring. Soon, as a further outgrowth of the book's sensation and success, I was invited in 1966 to appear for a month in the legendary hungry i nightclub in San Francisco. I had long been an outspoken advocate of the church's need to involve itself in the life and concerns of the world. Here was my ultimate chance to prove it.

Comedian and activist Dick Gregory headlined the show at the hungry i. We had met in Chicago

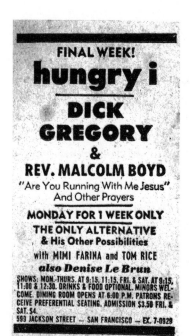

When I appeared with Dick Gregory at the hungry i in San Francisco for a month, the reaction was like a bombshell. I had a blast and enjoyed it, but was absolutely exhausted when the run ended.

when we were jailed together during a civil rights demonstration. I read prayers from *Are You Running with Me, Jesus?* and answered questions from members of the audience, engaging in a freewheeling dialogue. The *New York Times* reported one question I was asked and my response to it: "'Are you bringing Jesus to the hungry i?' a patron in the basement establishment of Enrico Banducci asked the cleric. 'How can I?' he replied. 'He's already in the hungry i.'"

Of course, this is the question everyone asked: What is a priest doing in the hungry i? I was consciously trying to slash through the utterly false, dreary, pretentious, theologically unsound, burdensome dichotomy between "church" and "world."

Performing at the hungry i meant as much to me as my involvement in such other key events as: participating in the freedom ride, reading my prayers to jazz accompaniment with guitarist Charlie Byrd at the Newport Jazz Festival, appearing in coffeehouse theaters in the plays that I wrote about racial justice, doing a reading of poetry in Cleveland with Langston Hughes, and being arrested while preaching a sermon during a peace mass inside the Pentagon.

What did I feel? I sensed there were flashing, agonizing, confusing images between people in the audience and me. I wondered: Could they see me as another human being or only as "Father," seated on a high stool in the hard light? Major newspapers and magazines from around the world sent journalists to report and interpret the performance; camera crews came from all the TV networks. I was intrigued, and sometimes frightened, by the uproar that ensued. All I was doing was trying to annihilate what I believed was an unnecessary and unfortunate separation between religion and life.

The first time my name was announced and I walked out from the back of the dark, crowded room onto the small stage, I was frightened. It reminded me of how I'd felt back in 1961, boarding a freedom ride bus. My mouth was dry, my heart pounding. I didn't know what was going to happen, yet I was committed to a course of action.

Each night—in fact, each of the two or three shows every night Monday through Thursday, and the three on Friday and Saturday—held its own mysteries. The late shows could be the best. One Sunday morning at around three A.M., when I was still on-stage, I realized how, for many of the people in that particular audience, this was church. It was so quiet you could hear a pin drop. A few players, actresses and actors from various San Francisco shows, had come in and put their feet up on the stage, and a kind of community naturally developed.

Each show had to represent, I felt, a whole new breakthrough from religion to life. Each audience was new, so it had its own hang-ups about a priest sitting on a bar stool and talking in a nightclub, a clerical collar up there under the amber light, frank talk in the name of God about sex and race, and finding new reality instead of escapism inside a San Francisco pleasure district. I would get waves of reaction from people, whether in strong silence or loud applause, sudden laughter, or a hushed reaction to something I had just said.

My awareness of a rapidly expanding biblical and theological illiteracy, coupled with the church's defensive posture of withdrawing farther and farther from the sights and smells of real life, had led me to seek new tasks in Christian communication. My appearance at the hungry i was one of those attempts.

A bread-and-butter issue for me was the question: How can the Christian faith be communicated? Indeed, is it often communicated inadvertently and outside the pale of self-conscious efforts to do so? And, by the same token, does it frequently elude all sorts of ambitious and even well-meaning attempts to communicate it?

For example, I found Federico Fellini's films *La Strada* and *La Dolce Vita* to be far more religious in content than Cecil B. DeMille's literalistic and shallow *The Ten Commandments*. Early on, theater touched my life when I was privileged to see Lee J. Cobb in the initial Broadway production of *Death of a Salesman*, Marlon Brando and Jessica Tandy in *A Streetcar Named Desire*, and the legendary Laurette Taylor in *The Glass Menagerie*. All this was food for my soul. Turning to the world of opera, Flagstad and Melchior in *Tristan und Isolde* (from the Met via radio broadcast) seduced me into becoming an opera lover when I was in junior high in Colorado. Live recitals by John Charles Thomas, Lawrence Tibbett, Marian Anderson, and Lotte Lehman followed—and I was a convert for life. Later I was present for Leontyne Price's *Aida*, the *Peter Grimes* of Jon Vickers and the Maria Callas *Tosca*, Montserrat Caballé's *Norma*, and Birgit Nilsson in Wagner's *Ring*. Over the years I've found in the arts an element of *praeparatio evangelica* when life is honestly portrayed, problems are stated, and people are offered some light, even shown some touch of glory, in the very life they are living.

Society itself is in flux. Rules have become blurred: sexual, political, ethical. Language as we've known it—the released Watergate tapes afforded the best evidence of this—has fallen into disuse. Attention time is brief. Idols and ideas alike are given a short run in the celebrity arena. "Speed" is the mercurial arbiter. Confusion and change exist where once there was at least a religious center of reference and awe, if not belief. Familiar words, phrases, and images had their place in a commonly accepted lexicon and folklore. This is no longer the case.

Against the background of such inescapable realities of life, my appearance at the hungry i took place. Was it possible to construct new bridges of feeling and encounter between the audience and me? I drove myself to the edge of physical and emotional exhaustion during that month. I wish that I had been able to continue and take the act on a national tour, visiting many cities and towns. I feel the experiment in communication was an honest and vital one.

It is ironic, I think, that my first book, written back in 1957, was entitled *Crisis in Communication*. Always communication with other people, either one-on-one or in a crowd, had been difficult for me. It was still when I appeared at the hungry i. I used to be afraid of serendipity and surprise; I needed a solid structure to lean on. Now I am no longer obsessed by what is linear. The flow of life beckons, and I am not afraid to follow it.

Yet another turning point emerged when, in 1977, I made the announcement that I am a gay man. At the time, this was controversial, because old attitudes had not yet changed. By now, they have to a greater degree than I could have imagined. I enjoy an integrated, balanced life. I am most grateful for it.

It is shared with my life partner of nearly twenty years, Mark Thompson. He writes books too. A team of writers under the same roof seems a bit like having two alchemists living and working in a medieval cottage. Edith Wharton wrote in *A Backward Glance*: "The real marriage of true minds is for any two people to possess a sense of humor or irony pitched in exactly the same key, so that their joint glances on any subject cross like interarching searchlights."

Mark and I have learned that patience, empathy, and humor are key factors in our life together. And we've managed to change in remarkable ways in response to each other. Younger than me, Mark is a classic "old soul," so in many instances he seems older than me. On the other hand, the child in me stays much alive. A *New York Times* book reviewer once called me "a balding Holden Caulfield"—the rebellious protagonist of J. D. Salinger's novel *Catcher in the Rye*. A balance that Mark and I find between these characteristics successfully marks our relationship.

An example of this occurred the day two new chairs appeared in the living room of our house. Mark got them. Uncharacteristically, and especially for as big a deal as this, he did not tell me he was buying the chairs until after he'd bought them. He broke the news by saying he had something to tell me. It seems he had come upon two wonderful chairs on sale—half price—and purchased them on the spot. If he had not acted quickly, he explained, they would have been picked up by someone else. He knew I would like them when I'd see them on delivery.

Mark and I were at home when the chairs arrived. I could see two delivery men at the foot of the outdoor stairway, struggling to get the chairs through an impossibly narrow space. They failed. Mark carried a ladder down the stairs, and the men managed to get the chairs onto the tile roof of the garage. Then they managed to carry them in a circuitous route up to our front door.

My childlike curiosity was already in full play: What would the chairs look like when they took their place in the room? They were covered in dark leather, and I saw immediately they were expansive enough to accommodate two first-class passengers flying to London on Virgin Airways. They might also be seen as two giant twins snuggled closely together. I welcomed them warmly and chose which one would be mine.

> I never liked masks, God,
> yet used to feel
> forced to wear them
>
> I lived two different
> parts of life
> seemingly split down
> the middle of my being
>
> let my naked face
> be seen by others
> as it is seen
> by you, God,
>
> let me look upon
> the naked faces of others
> in their natural beauty
> instead of painted masks
> that obscure truth
>
> thank you, God,
> for moving me
> openly into wholeness
> away from secrets and shadows

"Gay" used to stand for pretense and patterned choreography, playing prescribed roles and wearing masks. "Make it gay" was the watchword. It meant "put on the ritz," "keep the act going," "don't let down your guard," "keep on smiling," especially to conceal your sadness.

But there has been a change. Gay now means a new honesty. Where it used to signify wearing a mask, now it is a call to take off the masks. Its definition has shifted from form to content, sheer style to reality.

So, gay has something of universal meaning to say to everybody. Take off the masks of repressed anger, self-pity, sexual deceit, hypocrisy, social exploitation, and spiritual arrogance. Let communication be an event that involves people, not a charade of puppets. Be yourself. Relate to other selves without inhibition and pretense. Help others to be themselves too.

The journey toward self-honesty includes the study of one's myths. Everybody has them, including you and me. Since we invariably create many of our personal myths, it should not be extraordinarily difficult for us to perceive them honestly.

Also, most of us have painstakingly constructed our own masks, the ones that we wear and change ritualistically as we move from one situation to another, from this relationship to that. To take off the masks is to stop the ritual and let life replace it.

What happens to a person whose mask has been shed? Speaking for myself, I feel better than ever before. I acknowledge the mystery of my creation and my own mission within it. The reality of myself, as a person created in God's image, is openly shared.

I have learned that a mask obscures deep truths and gets in the way of life. Wearing a mask makes it harder to be an authentic person who engages others in the reality of living.

I suppose the final turning point, aging, is already a reality in my life. At present I fit any standard definition of growing older. Often my body so informs me. And, yes, there are moments when my energy of soul seems drained. Nevertheless, I possess a strong personal faith and a robust sense of humor. They help me immeasurably to remain hopeful, optimistic, and essentially passionate about the human experience.

Time *is* running out for me. I will not be here. How do I feel about this? There is a certain uneasiness when I think of leaving what is familiar and, indeed, all I know. I have loved life intensely, plunged into its midst, tasted its rough madness as well as its lovely sweetness. However, while I continue to love life, I've slowly and gradually begun to take a closer look at eternity, which extends beyond it. I find a beguiling touch of anticipation here. I am on the brink of something absolutely new happening to me.

Meanwhile, I have discovered problems that I must deal with in the present: in particular, ones related to health. (Any age has its own kinds of these, as you must know.) One of my problems—to my surprise—is found in my esophagus. For all I'd known, this word might mean an ancient Egyptian burial site. Now I learned (pain was my instructor) that it's located between my throat and stomach. I felt such agony that I was ready to visit a nearby hospital emergency room, until too-graphic recollections of the TV show *ER* kept me away. Instead I was helped by a change of diet, coupled with a fresh resolution to deal more effectively with stress.

Like many older men, I experienced problems with my prostate. An overzealous urologist suggested "immediate surgery." I decided against Western medical practice, however, and began using an herb called saw palmetto. Now I am fine.

Then, without warning, my right knee started to cause me considerable pain. It was difficult to walk. This new dilemma, caused by inflammation, was treated by medication and physical therapy. Yet the knee emerged again in a surreal experience when I visited friends in the country. On a late evening I walked outside their cottage to gaze at the stars in the night sky. Their lovely meadow was inviting, and I failed to take notice of an extremely high step that led from their porch to the yard. Losing balance, I plunged forward. Fortunately I did not resist the fall. And I fell in tall grass. While I hurt my fragile knee again, I had been extremely lucky. But I knew I should be far more careful in the future to avoid taking any kind of fall.

My eyes? Darth Vader was ready to strike in the guise of glaucoma. A conscientious eye physician, offering an excellent prescription, has kept this under control. Yet cataracts, like dark storm clouds, lurk on the horizon.

A major health problem is osteoarthritis. It requires a great deal of patience, faith, and hope. Let's see, do I have any more ailments? Oh yes, loss of memory. Difficulty remembering a word or recalling a name. (This is anything but a blessing for a writer.) Humor is a great helper.

My mentoring advice to someone younger about growing older? Simply *do* it, day at a time, hour at a time, moment at a time. Don't think about it too much. Make a conscious effort to learn how to do it instead of futilely worrying. Then, act on your new knowledge to the best of your ability. The best time to prepare for sixty, seventy, and eighty is when you are thirty, forty, or fifty.

The message? Take loving care of your body, mind, and soul. Be motivated. Cultivate passion. Keep exploring.

Chapter Six

UNDERSTANDING

I have been silent while the great autumn light begins; a time of change in the inner world.

—May Sarton

Forever getting ready for life instead of living it each day.

—Peter Matthiessen

I was young once, with desires, fears, needs, and anxiety that older people couldn't really understand where I was coming from.

Although I am approaching my eightieth birthday, I remain youthful in spirit, in soul, and with deep yearnings. From this vantage point, I feel a desire to share with others some of the significant lessons I've learned during my life's journey up to now. These have nurtured my growth in understanding.

They have often occurred in the form of challenges. I've tried to accept these, confront and embrace them, and endeavor to figure out a way of dealing with them constructively and realistically.

Here are some of the challenges.

To try to see inherent humor, absurdity, or irony in any situation.

In other words, to retain the ability to laugh. I'm finding that the key is to laugh *with*, not *at*, a person or situation and to remember that I can be laughably funny too. We need to include ourselves in the joke.

Politics is very, very funny. People are very funny. Sex is funny. Actress Mae West added humor and self-mockery to sex with her classic lines: "Too much of a good thing can be wonderful" and "When I'm good, I'm very good, but when I'm bad, I'm better."

A put-on accent (mock-royal, cockney, Charleston) is funny. A fur stole on a hot day is very funny. An overblown, atrocious production of the opera *Aida* is very, very funny.

Is it clear whether we are laughing at, or with, another person? Maybe the other person can sense, through our facial expressions and the strange noises of laughter, what we really feel. Our laughter process has been not funny at all when it has indulged in cruel stereotypes.

The best laugh includes us all. One morning I was having a cup of coffee in a big hotel where a Shriners convention was in progress. I noticed the men's cylindrical red hats with black tassels and silver attachments. I thought to myself, How odd. Soon I noticed some of the Shriners, wearing their hats, looking over at *me*, wearing an Episcopal priest's round, white clerical collar. Suddenly, we all broke into laughter. It grew and grew, including all of us. Under our outer differences, we were very much the same.

Part of the great fun of Hollywood in the golden era was its somewhat innocent craziness. I was so young. I can hardly believe myself as I was then. Funny, self-important and glamorous men and women were all around me; we were making movies; and there was a startling innocence about it all. We had no idea we were actually influencing the world

At my home in the Hollywood Hills I was often a party host. A youthful Elizabeth Taylor attended one of my parties and posed beside one of my mother's oil paintings. (Her signature, B. Boyd, is in the lower left corner.)

in complex ways and making social history. We simply went to our jobs, laughed uproariously about life in the studios and the stars' antics, made more money than other people, dined in the fanciest restaurants, gave little thought to the future, and put existential meaning on hold. We would have considered it utterly preposterous that a Hollywood actor might ever dream of becoming President of the United States.

Once I had been knocking myself out all week on a deadline assignment at the film studio where I worked. No end to the pressure was in sight. I was tired, frustrated, and mad. Nobody ever said thank-you. I decided to quit, but I'd do it my way. I telephoned one of the most expensive restaurants in Beverly Hills. Could I place an order for a dinner party at eleven P.M. for a hundred people on a sound-stage in the studio? There would be cocktails with hors d'oeuvres. After that, let's see—lobster, stuffed squab, Caesar salad, wine, chocolate truffles . . .

On the night of the dinner I roamed through the darkened studio and invited a Runyanesque assemblage, including janitors and guards. The tables were filled with guests dining by candlelight.

The next morning, on my arrival for work, a guard at the studio gate said the studio vice-president wanted to see me right away. "Hurry," he said. The vice-president seemed a man obsessed. His rage knew no limit. "You're fired!" he shouted. "No," my voice rang out. He stopped in his tracks. "I quit," I said. The next moments were certifiably insane. Although firing me no longer remained an option, he was impelled to exert his superiority and preserve his ego's dominance. So he offered me a huge raise. I accepted it. Later, I found it healing to laugh at myself.

To define success and failure, and learn how to live with each.
By some popular yardsticks, success is determined primarily by amounts of money received, possessions under control, name recognition (including notoriety), and how big a splash one has made in measurable waters. Failure is determined by minimal money and possessions, anonymity, low profile, and inability to "make a mark" (or disinterest in it).

I've long been instructed by the dark truth revealed in Edwin Arlington Robinson's poem "Richard Cory." Cory was rich, and "schooled in every grace."

> In fine, we thought that he was everything
>   To make us wish that we were in his place.

The denouement is that Richard Cory one night put a bullet through his head. He *wasn't* a success. He *wasn't* a role model. He *wasn't* "everything to make us wish that we were in his place."

Richard Cory, instead, was apparently a rather pathetic human being who suffered a great deal under a mask of success, placed a premium on public appearance, refused or found himself unable to deal with private demons, remained too proud and self-reliant to seek help, and chose role-playing over a genuine life with other real people. Wishing always to be larger than life, Richard Cory apparently didn't accept himself as a human being. He couldn't stand such limitations! Didn't he, after all, remain a perfectionist to the end?

I learned about the stark contrast between legiti-
mate success and failure early in my high school
days. Mine was a glamorous, upscale, privileged, and
snobbish school where "success" was earmarked for a
few beauty queens and jocks, "celebrity" was pack-
aged thereby, and top priority was placed on preparing for admission to socially exclusive colleges (with
the "best" sororities and fraternities), instead of academic advancement, social inclusivity, or cultural
awareness.

Consequently, I saw success and failure in
bizarre extremes all around me, and readily found
out how false these were. I learned firsthand that
self-worth, honest ambitions, and persistent adher-
ence to fundamental goals far outweighed mere
transitory trappings of success. This became an
invaluable lesson because, later in life when I had
to deal with my own experiences of failure and success in the most realistic and sometimes painful
ways, I was prepared.

Years later, I remember an occasion when my ego
was stroked by an invitation to address ten thousand people at a convention gathering that was
highly newsworthy and covered by national media.
It was an adrenalin high. Yet a far more significant
event, in terms of my own life, occurred shortly
afterward when I met with less than twenty people
in an inner-city church basement. It was far more
real, intimate, and relevant. While it was not a "success" by any worldly standard of measurement, it
was a genuine success in terms of my consciousness
and development.

To make and honor commitments.

As a child, I saw commitments torn asunder as I experienced a devastating divorce in my family, one fueled by alcoholism, adultery, and abandonment. Then my formative years were lived during the great American Depression of the '30s. It was a chaotic time of economic breakdown and psychological wounds. I can even remember going to bed hungry; mere survival took precedence over the niceties of life. The absence of security and a tangible structure of life made them ever more distant and remote. Just live for today became the byword. Seemingly one could not trust very much in any kind of future.

Coming to Hollywood out of college, I felt almost as if I were a gold miner in California in another century. Everything seemed to involve pure luck. There was gold in the hills: sacrifice anything for it! (The only law was survival of the fittest.) Abjure kindness or softness in climbing to the top; show no mercy; get your share. Ethics had no place here; morality was only a weapon to be bent. Time was gold itself, so either make it now—or never.

This was clearly not an environment in which one thought about making solid, lasting commitments of any kind. A job was seen primarily as a stepping-stone to another, better job in this Oz-like citadel of glamour, which had its good witches, bad witches, and wizards. The major task was: find the yellow brick road. But there were many detours, roadblocks, false exits, and conflicting signs. It became impossible to commit to reaching the Emerald City. Why? Because one had no idea where it was.

As a young man, I found myself torn to pieces

emotionally because I wanted, and needed, to make serious commitments. I asked myself how, or when, could I grow up? It seemed I was detached from real life, a mere observer of it. I was isolated over *here*. Life was in progress over *there*. Didn't I want to be caught up in the intensity and enormity of life, even if it cost me everything? My noninvolvement seemed almost too painful to stand. Yet still I appeared to wait. Didn't one have to lose one's life in order to save it? What could I do? My earlier life's experiences had taken their toll, making the idea of commitments very, very difficult for me.

Soon, however, when commitment to life itself summoned me in myriad ways, and I plunged into involvement at many levels, I was enormously grateful. Finally, I could relate positively to lines that had always called out to me from Robert Frost's poem "Stopping by Woods on a Snowy Evening":

> But I have promises to keep,
> And miles to go before I sleep.

To comprehend the diverse strands of life and understand oneself as a member of a vast family.

All of us, you and I, are individuals. We are also part of relationships and communities. We belong, in a sense, to a family or families, and to a job, a place, a profession or kind of work. We belong to a church, synagogue, mosque, or other kind of spiritual community, a neighborhood, a political party, a nation, certain ethnic bonds—a world.

We belong to ideas, certain ideas, a combination of them, and to dreams, a dream. We belong to such a network of things that it can be baffling. I want to share with you a very personal aspect of belonging that emerged in the complex network of my own life.

Three of my grandparents were Christians. The fourth, my maternal grandfather, was a Jew. (My grandmother's first husband was Harry Joseph. He died before I was born. Later, Grandma married for a second time.) During high school and college, Jewishness often seemed forbidding and even strange to me. What was kosher food? a bar mitzvah?

While I was still in high school, the specter of anti-Semitism came to the forefront of my mind. My worldview then included goose-stepping Nazis in shiny black boots. The staccato quality of Hitler's voice (I heard it on the radio) stuck in my awareness. It was accompanied by the rhythmic, measured cries from many thousands of his supporters' throats, growing in intensity and asking for blood.

Years passed. In seminary, when I prepared to become an Episcopal priest, I asked myself: Why must religion separate people instead of uniting them? Why must universal love give way, in the priorities of organized religion, to erecting high walls between people in whom God's love dwells? In my first parish, a small Orthodox synagogue was across the street. I was asked to turn on the light inside the synagogue early Saturday (Sabbath) mornings. I thereby became a *shabbos goy*, a Gentile who performs this sort of task for Jews who are not allowed to perform them.

Later, in the civil rights movement, I marched and went to jail with Jews. A rabbi with me said his participation was based on the teaching of the Torah that any and all suffering was his suffering, his con-

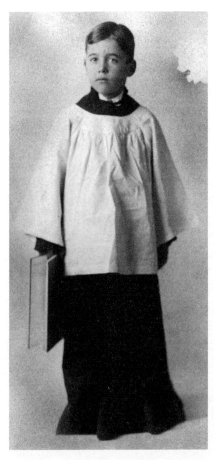

My whole life has been in the church. I sang in a choir until my voice changed. I was also a youthful acolyte who assisted in the liturgy. In college I assumed I'd become an atheist. Obviously I didn't.

cern. "Let justice roll down like waters," the prophet Amos cried. This recalled Jesus' words: "I was a stranger and you welcomed me, I was naked and you gave me clothing, I was sick and you took care of me, I was in prison and you visited me." In the early 1960s I visited Israel for the first time. When, in the early 1970s, I was invited to live in Jerusalem for three months at Mishkenot Sha'ananim, a center for writers and artists, it was a fresh experience to live by the Jewish clock: the Sabbath was Saturday, not Sunday. It began Friday afternoons, when everything stopped, life came to a halt, and the city grew quiet. Jewishness surrounded me. I liked going to the Israel Museum, spending hours there immersing myself in Jewish culture and history. But it was also on the streets, in the air, all about me. At Christmastime, I went to hear Handel's *Judas Maccabeus* instead of his *Messiah*, as I had usually done in the United States.

Living in Jerusalem I thought often of my Jewish grandfather, especially late one night when I stood silently before the Western Wall of the Temple of Solomon, the renowned "Wailing Wall" of prayer, which has long held deep meaning in Jewish history and consciousness. Floodlights illuminated its ancient stones. A figure dressed in black sat before the wall, chanting, his voice rising and falling.

I was aware that my grandfather had never visited here. I dug deep in spiritual roots as I meditated in the silence. I placed my forehead on a cold, ancient stone of the wall, offering thanks for my grandfather's life.

I have learned to be grateful for the diverse strands of life. They provide an essential networking that takes us outside ourselves into the great world. The human family is drawn together in the intimacy of what can be shared.

To communicate with someone else when it's almost impossible.
I've found this usually involves curbing my pride, getting myself out of the way as the supposed center

of the universe, and balancing self-interest with the common good. It is important to hear what is actually meant rather than what is simply said in words. Although people should say what they mean, often they don't. So it's important to observe expressions and actions as well as words.

It can be a big problem when my inability to engage in dialogue matches that of others. It is necessary to *listen* to someone else's point of view, *hear* it, *comprehend* it and try to *understand* it. Nothing is deadlier than I-I/me-me. Make it *we* and *us*. When words fail, coldness replaces warmth, silences become threatening. Familiar ways of bonding are met with indifference. While alienation grows, vulnerability is painful. This is a time to be quiet and wait. If ever there was a time to listen, *this* is it. Be ready to respond to communications the other person initiates.

Misreading signs of human behavior can have serious repercussions. Long ago I discovered that a seemingly unfriendly attitude may indicate nothing more than, say, a toothache or a troubled life at home. Appearances can be deceptive. We assume: This person couldn't possibly cheat. (But she does.) That relationship is more solid than the Rock of Gibraltar. (It isn't.) Pat, the well-groomed, smiling man, is obviously very bright, while Mike, the thrown-together one, is a dolt. (The reverse is true.) So we need to look for the real (not the assumed) person behind the stranger we meet.

It never ceases to amaze me that some people offhandedly tell such outright lies as: "I like it." "Your job is safe." "I'll be back in five minutes." They say things they don't mean. The result is hurt, confusion, and resentment. Saying what we mean keeps confusion to a minimum. At a recent meeting I attended, a dozen professional women and men gathered to draft a statement about long-range plans. The discussion grew ever more abstract and unrealistic. Finally, I asked: "Why don't we say what we mean?" A silence fell. Then someone laughed sheepishly and said, "But that's so hard to do." Yet it's much harder not to do it.

The biggest problem in communication is not knowing the message that's needed, whether it's "I love you" or "I'm worried you're stabbing me in the back." The key is: we need to understand what must be communicated. Too often we tell people what we think they ought to know instead of finding out what they need to know.

Communication is in the present. This moment—now—might change our life forever. This may be our only chance to communicate with a particular person.

One of my favorite news clips of all time was written early in the last century. It concerned the first two automobiles ever to have appeared on the streets of a major American city. The opening sentence went like this: "The only two automobiles in town collided today at the intersection of State and Main." It isn't just cars that collide. People do, all the time, in families, jobs, social relationships, and the public arena.

I've had my share of human collisions. I don't want more of them. They are painful, confusing, costly, ugly—and can be avoided. How? By communicating clearly, honestly, effectively, and caringly. Even then, all the problems of communicating will not have been solved, because misunderstandings fester, various people have various emotional or psychological problems, and ancient wounds require seemingly endless healing. Yet, underneath it all, I have found that the secret of being heard is, for the most part, simply to listen.

To accept change and struggle as integral parts of life.

I like James Broughton's poem "Junior's Struggle": "Now I lay me down to sleep. But keep me awake, Lord, keep me awake!"

We need to be awake if we are to make needed changes in the quality of the Earth's life and support peace and justice for its people. I've found myself caught between my beliefs and the kind of world I was born in. So I *had* to act! This, despite an innate shyness, a lazy streak, and an overwhelming desire to place *being* ahead of *doing*. Yet I couldn't stand back in a posture of meditative repose and not be active in bringing about whatever needed changes seemed possible. At certain moments the explosions and cries in the world have seemed to echo inside the whirling universe of my own mind. Other times I have seemed to wander aimlessly inside the world, scaling its heights or exploring its valleys.

I do not believe it is possible, barring a lobotomy of one's senses and feelings, to "get away from it all." I do not want to get away from it. Any selfish attempt to escape from human and ecological realities is doomed by moral as well as pragmatic facts of life.

How do I find peace amid the wars inside and out-side myself? Invariably I seek a perspective of life that bursts loose from the limitations and imprisoning ghettos confined to my own experience.

For example, I struggle with all the energy I can summon to extend my thinking and feeling beyond stultifying categories that would strangle promise and hope, incarnate cynicism and despair, and deny the holiness in ordinary life. I have learned that, in order to achieve necessary and new levels of identity as a human being, I must fight against programmed existence. So I must enter streams of consciousness, essentially by means of deeper human experiences and relationships, that shatter rigidities within my own thought and spiritual patterns.

Yes, this can be painful. This is one of its virtues, for it wars against a self-induced and socially manip-ulated kind of tranquilizing. I struggle to survive and grow by reminding myself, in a dozen, a hundred, a thousand ways, that I am a person. This immediately involves me in the world of people.

People are changing all the time. This involves me in change.

People are struggling from birth to death to sur-vive, work, believe, hope, and love. This involves me in struggle.

To welcome the unexpected.

Invariably, the four seasons help me to do this.

Autumn means anticipation for me. It is a restless time, in which I am restless.

What is to come? There will be snow and ice, spring and next summer, but what else? Autumn is a signpost that reminds me there will always be mystery and the unknown in life.

My own life, which has seemingly been progressing in a somewhat predictable way on steady supports, may suddenly swerve in a wholly new direction. I may be called on to develop fresh attitudes, relationships, and skills, even become someone whom I would shortly not recognize.

Autumn announces life is mercurial, dynamic, and changing, and that a facade of security and sameness is an absurd delusion. Autumn speaks of mystery with a hint of danger.

Winter's first snowfall came last night. I heard the strange sound of its near silence when I awakened a few moments ago.

Outside my window is a fresh vision. I am grateful for the punctuation mark of this event in my life. I prepare to walk outside the house and embrace the snow: I will hold it in my hands, rub it on my face, let it melt in my mouth, and walk through soft drifts of it with my feet.

It is a challenge to make tracks in freshly fallen snow—symbolic of marks I must make on life itself. Why? Because I touch other people's lives. I hope my tracks in snow and life are clear.

Spring's miracle is happening again. Yesterday the air was still bitingly cold. Today it suggests seductive warmth. Walking just now I saw emerging buds.

I know, of course, that spring does not last. What shall I do with it during these brief, splendid days? I am content to move easily or stay quiet in its embrace, breathe its smell, and let the world stop for us. But it will not stop. Nor will I, running briefly across space and time.

The challenge of a summer's day is that too much adulthood, taken too seriously, needs revision.

I find myself on May Day at a country fair. A hand-lettered sign bears the words "Bleeding Heart. Blooms All Summer." People carry paper bags filled with fresh vegetables. Madrigal singers entertain. Hawkers sell clay flutes, while people dance on the green.

Dogs of all sizes and descriptions are everywhere. Cornish pastries, popovers, tarts of "fyne roasted chycken" are for sale at stalls. Signs point out Glassmakers Lane, Printmakers Way, and Candlemakers Cove.

A black goat wearing a straw hat ambles by. A dancer is about to follow a tumbling act. Women and men and children put on costumes and become all the exciting persons they've always wanted to be.

I sip ginger beer and burn my mouth eating a hot fruit tart. Someone flies a kite. I look at flags and banners of yellow, orange, blue, and red. Rolling hills and green slopes ease gently down to streams of water, where kids wade. Old trees resemble Sherwood Forest.

To live as fully as possible in the present moment.
Why has this been the most difficult challenge in my life? Instead of staying focused clearly on the here and now, the mind wanders off here, there, in myriad directions. Old tapes play—again, again—in one's head, creating distractions.

As the present becomes blurred and distant, it is easy to be seduced by withdrawal into the past, even when the terrain is strewn with hard stones, hellish to travel, and images it conjures are painful and disturbing.

I confess that I feel a sense of enormous relief when I am able to simply let go, permitting myself to find the height and depth of meaning *in this moment*. Slowly, I realize the past was once the present; the future, when experienced, becomes the present.

Indeed, the present moment has a lean ordinariness to it, along with wonder and grace. It is full of potential.

Yet why do many of us find certain moments garbed in mystery, epiphany, challenge, and a kind of exaltation, and, conversely, label other moments as despicably drab, inconsequential, colorless, and pedestrian? Our vision fails to absorb us on these latter occasions.

When this happens, we need to change our focus: to look within as well as outside; to perceive the reality of what essentially remains unseen; to allow a spectrum of colors as replacement for a monochrome; to catch a glimpse of wonder.

Growing older, I do not find it necessarily easier to live in the present moment, although I am more acutely conscious of it. I need to make the most of it, relish it, bask in it, celebrate it, find satisfaction and peace in it, and accept its human limitation for me.

At the outset of this book, I stated its major themes: Learning, Remembering, Simplifying, Maturing, Exploring, and Understanding. How does my own life stack up in relation to these?

Learning is never completed. I remain an eternal student, incomplete and unfulfilled, gazing at a full range of Mount Everests of the mind that remain unclimbed.

Remembering is, I am aware, a selective process. There are certain things one wishes not to remember, others that one chooses to remember in contexts and patterns that are attractive and familiar. My memory seems to defy any easy description. On the one hand, it's a universe with its own moons, stars, and planets; then it's a huge castle packed to the gills with objects of all sizes and kinds; but perhaps most often, it's a live echo chamber.

Simplifying has been, and is, my greatest challenge. I like to cut a Gordian knot when I can, work my way through human spiderwebs, clean out cluttered spaces and dank closets, and live by acknowledging priorities and granting their frights. Simplicity, for me, is the greatest beauty. There is a certain humility in simplicity that allows access and invites dialogue.

Maturing? I leave this to others. I can't possibly say how mature I have become.

Exploring? Yes, I have been, and remain, an avid and intrepid explorer. I firmly believe that always there are new spaces to explore, bridges to cross, hills to climb, oceans to sail, puzzles to confront. Once on a visit to Baku I dined in a caravansary where Marco Polo was said to have stayed. I enjoyed such proximity to him, despite the separation of centuries; he remains a role model par excellence.

We come, finally, to the category of Understanding. *What* do I understand? Something of laughter. Of pain. Of forgiveness. Of human imperfection and ambiguity. Of tragedy. Of joy. Of structure and change. Of tears. Of hope. Of love.

My understanding changes deeply when it comes to faith. Faith encompasses my understanding, and then moves beyond it. Faith is the ground I stand on, the air I breathe, the thread of life that connects me to continuing life with God in eternity.

Barefoot, I walk in the surf.

The ocean sounds like the world's symphony orchestras gathered in concert, with bursts of trumpets here, nuances of cellos there.

My footprints in the sand are wiped out instantly by a fresh wave, yet the water cannot efface my shadow. It remains constant. I venture farther and farther out as the tide seems to recede, but now an unexpected strong wave hits me, nearly knocking me down.

The child in me, who was denied a happy childhood, is having one today. I laugh easily as I run. A piece of seaweed is stuck between my toes. Beyond the expanse of white sand—here on a deserted beach at Big Sur on the California coast—lies a small canyon filled with windswept cypresses.

Looking out at the bay, I see an immense wave break with gentle fury over an ancient rock. Sky seems infinite, ocean limitless, a foretaste of eternity.

Sun is warm on my face and arms, chest and thighs.

I feel whole in this moment—in heart and mind, soul and body.

I feel free: playful and serious, old and young, struggling with life and content with it, painfully aware of problems and immensely grateful for peace.